MANAGING
YOUR
STRENGTHS

MANAGING

YOUR

STRENGTHS

ALLAN KATCHER PH.D. &

KENNETH PASTERNAK

This book was printed in the United States of America.

To order additional copies of this book, contact:
Xlibris Corporation
1-888-795-4274
www.Xlibris.com
Orders@Xlibris.com
16554-KATC

Contents

ACKNOWLEDGMENTS

This book was not only the collaborative product of Katcher and Pasternak, but in a sense, the collaboration of many people.

Our inspirational forefathers were Eric Fromm, Carl Rogers and Peter Drucker. Fromm's emphasis on the strength-management paradox, the value of intense understanding and acceptance stressed by Carl Rogers, and Drucker's insistence that management is an attitude as much as a set of techniques provided the foundation for the LIFO® Method.

Stuart Atkins was a co-developer and originator of many LIFO® concepts – his book *The Name of Your Game*, was the first one to depict the fruitful possibilities of LIFO® applications. He has been an enthusiastic and inspirational colleague – who still remains a receptive listener to new ideas.

Over the years, our LIFO® agents have worked with ideas, conducted seminars with millions of people and made their own special contributions: Ian Tibbles in theoretical development, Jan De Jong in computer assessments and negotiation training, Linda Wiens and Cliff McIntosh for many integrations with FIRO-B and other style systems, Betty Forbis for her intuitive and deep portrayals of individual styles, Birger Bertheussen for his innovative experiments in educational methodology, Rene Bergermaier for his systemic focus on improving concepts and the development of an Austro-German community of LIFO® analysts, and all of the LIFO® agents who have committed themselves to the advancement of our values.

A special debt is owed to Business Consultants Inc., who began working with The LIFO® Method 29 years ago. They took the risk of introducing workshops and seminars to their clients, became strong endorsers and innovators and have provided 750,000 Japanese Managers with LIFO® insights about individual, team and organizational development. They recently demonstrated their commitment by purchasing Allan Katcher International, Inc., and Stuart Atkins Inc. to create a global LIFO® business. We are deeply grateful for their accomplishments and encouragement, as well as the special support of Shogo Saito.

Larry Katcher made a brilliant LIFO® analysis of the Beatles and has written perceptive reviews of several competitive style systems. These have turned out to be quite popular and we value highly these original contributions. These, along with 100 other articles on the LIFO® Method, can be viewed on the Internet (*www.bcon-lifo.com*). Andrew Katcher and Ken Finn designed the first LIFO® computer-assisted report system that has provided a major tool for individual and group analyses.

Our family colleagues Gloria Katcher and Harriet Nyholm-Pasternak have not only endured our participation in so many events away from home but have also helped make our ideas clearer and more "user friendly." Gloria Katcher conducted successful training seminars in Mexico and Spain and also provided the original Spanish translations of our materials.

Special thanks is due to Cecilia Bergamini, the pioneering Brazilian agent, who was responsible for getting our first LIFO® book published.

Finally, we have to reconfirm the old adage "by your pupils you are taught." Certainly, encounters with thousands of participants have created new insights and led to the development of ideas and explanations that are more rigorous and practical. Thanks to all of you.

INTRODUCTION

THE LIFO® METHOD

The term LIFO® stands for "Life Orientations." Orientations are patterns of goals, attitudes, beliefs and behaviors that influence how we cope with situations under normal and stressful circumstances. As a result of our life experiences and learning, each of us develops a unique and characteristic profile or set of orientations.

If we were automobiles, most of us would be using much less of the engine capacity available under our hoods. When driving, many of us miss opportunities to change lanes, we sometimes race our engines more than is needed for the terrain we're covering, or we don't realize when it is time to shift gears. Ultimately, we may even rush to buy a new model before realizing the full worth of the old investment.

Bob is a manager who by all accounts does a creditable job. He is dedicated, conscientious and hardworking. When offered a promotion, Bob declines, saying he doubts that he could perform at that higher level.

Tom is a dynamic, hard charging salesman. He is accustomed to overcoming resistance with smart answers. Tom promotes himself for a new job, gets it, but fails because he tries too hard and he doesn't allow members of his staff to exercise their talents.

Bob is unsure about his own capabilities and cuts himself off from an exciting new opportunity. Tom is overconfident and fails to recognize the potential contributions of others.

Jane is an accountant who runs her financial group according to written policies and procedures. She carefully checks all reports and systematically follows up every task that is assigned. When change is required, she adapts slowly, thereby incurring impatience and disapproval from her boss. She's guilty of over-doing a good thing and not recognizing when to modify her approach.

Betty handles relationships smoothly and with ease. Her public relations department has been responsible for several successful advertisement campaigns and adept handling of consumer confidence issues. Yet, when things were getting out of hand while working on a PR campaign for a key client, she optimistically portrayed events as being under control. When that was found not to be the case, her false assurances ultimately destroyed the credibility of the company.

From the LIFO® perspective described in this book, these cases reveal a failure to manage strengths: that is, we fail to manage our strengths when we either *under*—or *over*-utilize our own strengths or when we don't combine our personal skills with those of others in order to obtain synergistic output. This book tells you how to make more of yourself than you have realized is possible by exploring the possibilities of managing strengths. In terms of our car analogy, you will learn how to unleash the full horse-power that you possess.

All good managers understand the importance of knowing and appreciating their resources. In business these resources are money, people, systems, technologies and history. In a person, they are skills, talents, beliefs, values, experience and knowledge. To be effective managers we must begin, therefore, by knowing ourselves, valuing our strengths, understanding our impacts, appreciating our successes and recognizing our failures.

In reviewing the nature of human character, Erich Fromm, in his book *Man For Himself*, calls attention to a surprising paradox. He writes, "Our weaknesses are often the excessive use of our strengths." Thus confidence can lead to brashness, caution to procrastination, diplomacy to distorting the truth, modesty to self-deprecation. Implied in Fromm's paradox is the notion that our strengths and weaknesses are simply separate ends of the same continuum. To be effective we have to recognize how we are performing and learn to assess where we are on this continuum of behavior. Hence, the LIFO® Method emphasizes strength management®.

This book will help you learn to recognize and appreciate the behavioral continuum on which you and others operate, and to seek ways in which you can combine your strengths with those of others for mutual benefit.

We will also show you how to use five basic strategies for successful strength management: **Accentuate the positive** ("confirming"), *De-emphasize* **the negative** ("moderating"), **Appreciate others** ("augmenting"), **Bridge the gaps** ("bridging), and **Keep your eyes open to change** ("extending"). You will see how you can use these approaches for improving interpersonal communications, team-building, managing conflict, coping with stress, and managing time.

Managing effectively however, requires a discipline. One distinguished vice-president said, "You can't manage anything unless you can control it. And you can't control anything unless you measure it." It's not enough to have good intentions, you have to achieve and observe what you're doing so you can change if you're not getting the results you want.

In later chapters we will discuss a simple model that will help you to manage your relationships with others by examining your intentions, observing your behaviors and measuring the success of your impact on people and tasks. When you combine this kind of analysis with strength management® you will see how you can improve your effectiveness.

In the next chapter, you will start to learn how to recognize the strengths you have, how they are similar to yet different from others. You will also learn about an important variation of the golden rule – the LIFO® Rule: "**Do unto others as they would like to be done to!**"

—

In summary, the LIFO® Method will enable you to see that

- We learn to behave towards each other in ways that seem best to satisfy our different psychological and physical needs for self-fulfilment. This behavior becomes our natural or "preferred" orientation towards other people.
- This preferred orientation represents the source of our strengths which – when we are able to understand, develop and manage them – can be even more productive in satisfying our needs.
- The combination of behavioral orientations that make up our behavioral style is not, however, infallible in satisfying needs. When our strengths are carried to excess they can be counterproductive. They become, in fact, our weaknesses.
- This tendency for our strengths to be used in excess becomes most counter-productive as our environment is affected by conditions of stress and of conflict.

Through the LIFO® Method we can free ourselves from styles of behavior that frustrate our basic goal of self-fulfilment and devise options for managing situations more effectively.

CHAPTER 1

UNLEASHING YOUR POWER TO CHANGE

Each and every day we are affected by changes in our business or personal circumstances. We experience these changes in the ways we work with our staff, bosses, and colleagues; at home in the ways we relate to our partners and children; and generally in how we try to cope with daily demands and problems. The pressures of change are constant.

For some, personal change means putting on different masks depending on the situation. You might achieve successful results by behaving differently as a *manager*, as a *parent*, and then again as a *spouse*. For many this gives an overriding sense that they are not being true to themselves, even a feeling that they are directing or manipulating others. Life can be difficult if you were to pass the whole day trying to be the projection of what you want people to believe about you. For some, this approach can even lead to a loss of self-identity. Have you ever heard a friend say, "I don't recognize who I am anymore"?

When people wish to change, it usually means that they recognize they are not getting fulfilling results from their interpersonal relationships. Often they are not happy with themselves. Pained by feelings of inadequacy or self-doubt, they frequently turn to personal development programs or self-help books. In doing so the first thing they usually encounter are the very *weaknesses* that made them unsuccessful or unhappy to begin with.

The **LIFO® Method** was developed because there is a more

comfortable and productive way to develop your interpersonal and communication skills – and ultimately to feel more satisfied with yourself.

The LIFO® Method affirms there can't be only one way or model to help people change. If there were, wouldn't this lead to everyone becoming a copy of another? The father-in-law of one of the authors often said, "all people are born as originals but sadly, most people do die as copies." Fortunately, history is full of examples of people who have achieved success using many different behaviors and styles.

Think of Abraham Lincoln, Mahatma Gandhi, and Margaret Thatcher in government and politics, and in the business world, Tom Watson, Bill Gates and Jack Welch. Each of these figures has used an individual style to achieve success in his or her chosen fields of excellence, and each is clearly not a copy of any other. What would have happened if each of these people had to fit into a standard model of behavior?

When development seminars and books suggest that people change, they usually offer an approach for how you can be more effective. Typically, successful people are offered as examples and you are asked to look at what they do, how they go about getting results, and what behavioral characteristics they display in doing so. Their observable skills are separated into stages or steps. Their behavioral and personality characteristics are defined. You are then encouraged to try to emulate those behaviors in order to develop into the manager or leader you currently are not. All too often you receive little help in how to incorporate these behaviors into your current style and how, in fact, you really can make them work effectively.

The complexity of interpersonal relations is often over simplified. Little credence is given to the fact that we tend to operate across a range of behaviors depending on circumstances. In addition, many self-help books do not take into account that people often operate differently depending upon the person with whom they are dealing or their own level of comfort in a given situation. It is seldom emphasized that there are many paths that can lead to success. The fact that there may be diverse and equally effective methods for dealing with situations gets lost in what sometimes appear to be a formulaic approach to improving ourselves and our interpersonal relationships.

Finally, behavioral improvement texts often ask us to identify and examine our weaknesses. For some this is not an easy thing to do. How objective are we about our weaknesses? Many theories emphasize that if we can work on those weaknesses by observing successful leaders, we can overcome problems and achieve success ourselves.

There are some serious flaws in this whole process:

- If you are going to spend a lot of time blaming yourself for what you are not, you are going to waste a precious amount of your life trying to be someone other than yourself.
- It is not likely that you are going to find the perfect model of behavior to follow that fits you.

You do not have to read books on psychology to know that each person is different and unique. Personal comfort starts with becoming aware of and having respect for this uniqueness. From a LIFO® point of view, we find that people may do the same thing in different ways for different reasons, yet all achieve results.

On the other hand, you can also see that no one is perfect and it is not possible to be all things to all people. If it were possible to repair each of our natural defects, a perfect human being would be created. It is unlikely that such perfection would be "human" any more.

The Strength Management® emphasis in this book represents a first step for those who are interested in personal development. Strength Management® helps you put in order what you know about yourself. For the sake of personal growth and change it is absolutely essential to know your strengths. You just cannot build on weaknesses; you must build on the solid foundation of your existing strengths.

You are probably thinking, "This process can't be all that easy." You are right. However, we need not feel that we are simply ordained to be what we are. We do have the power to modify the way we behave.

We are not likely to change radically from one extreme to another. First efforts to change will probably be simple modifications as might be observed in the change of an annoying habit. The more success you have with a "new" behavior, the more positive regard it will get from others and yourself, and the more the behavior will be seen as a part of you.

It is important that you develop your own criteria for measuring success. Nothing can be more discouraging than to hear others respond to your self perceived changes with remarks like, "I really haven't noticed any difference" or "Yes, I've seen it, but so what?" The more you value yourself and the progress you are making in your relationships, the more your "rewards" will be the achievement of your own personal goals and your increasing sense of self-worth.

While undertaking such efforts at change, it is important to believe that you are not merely your past behavior, but *a work in the process of change*, directed by your own desires and practices. It is positive regard for yourself and appreciation of your strengths that creates the potential for change.

This book has been written as a means to share this valuable tool for business managers and anyone who seeks to improve his or her ability to work with others. The LIFO® Method focuses on managing your strengths – to provide strategies for making use of what already works for you and to use the strengths of others to complement your own. It begins with a description of our basic ways for coping with our lives, many illustrations of how and why people are different, strategies for developing better relationships, and techniques for managing self and teams for productive outcomes. After reading this book you will immediately be able to apply new approaches and strategies to your relationships at work and elsewhere.

CHAPTER 2

THE LIFO® METHOD – A DIFFERENT WAY

The LIFO® method starts from the point of view that we need to understand and build from our ***strengths***, rather than get mired in a discouraging review of our weakness. All people naturally develop a range of styles (or orientations) for how they interact with others, whether in the workplace or in our private lives. Our tendency is to continue to use those behaviors that have been the most successful for us in the past. These become our self-perceived or self-selected strengths. We continue to rely on these strengths when we are working with others in daily life – whether we are functioning under normal situations or when stress levels are high. In stressful situations it is natural to fall back on approaches that have worked well for us in the past or those that we are most comfortable using. Unfortunately, using our strongest behaviors at the wrong time or to the wrong extent can bring us the least effective results.

The LIFO® approach acknowledges that we are not simple organisms that can just choose new behaviors to add to our personal tool kits. We are complicated beings that possess a blend of different behaviors and styles. Each of us has some styles that are more dominant or prevalent than others. Equally important is that we are often not aware that our behaviors fall into patterns that can be predicted and understood. This is good news. If we can understand how we tend to behave under certain conditions, we can, firstly, start the process to change our behavior; and secondly, we can interpret other people's behaviors more easily. The combination of these two aspects, knowing ourselves and understanding others, will enable us to begin building new strategies for improving our interpersonal skills and achieving greater success in communicating, selling, negotiating and managing.

SOME THINGS YOU SHOULD KNOW ABOUT IT

- The LIFO® method is grounded in the *academic theory* and clinical research of several important practitioners from the fields of psychology and management practice including Kurt Lewin, Carl Rogers, Erich Fromm, and Peter Drucker.
- Stuart Atkins and Allan Katcher, both practising psychologists, created the LIFO® Method over 30 years ago based on their practical experience in directing management development programs for multinational companies.
- LIFO® thinking and processes have been continually researched and updated. More than 8.0 million people based in small and large companies in 26 countries have participated in LIFO® training.

THE UTILITY OF LIFO® APPROACHES

The LIFO® Method is one of the best-kept secrets for helping people improve their effectiveness in working with others (although so many people have been exposed to it). How will it help you achieve greater success?

- You will gain **instant realization** of who you are in a *positive* way. With that knowledge you will learn how to deal more effectively with others.

- The LIFO® method provides what we call a **"periodic table" of behaviors.** You may recall from basic studies in chemistry the periodic table that groups elements. It provides an excellent analogy for us. Knowing where an element is placed on the table enables us to understand its properties and how it will interact with other elements. In much the same way, the LIFO® approach will help you to understand why and how you deal with people in certain ways and why others may react differently from your expectations.

- All of us have talents within us that often are untapped. LIFO® thinking shows you how to **tap resources within you** and to manage them in order to improve communications and relationships.

- All of the elements described above not only provide benefits to individuals, but also improve the way teams are formed and how they function.

- The LIFO® method offers especially effective tools to assist you in many day-to-day tasks. For example, one executive was trying to make up his mind whether a young manager was able to handle greater responsibilities. He used LIFO® techniques to confirm his perceptions about the manager. Furthermore, he was able to use his insights to talk about these perceptions with the manager in everyday language. The method does not introduce pretentious or obscure scientific terminology.

- Another senior executive was trying to determine why members of his team were not getting along as well as he had hoped. He was able to use LIFO® concepts to understand why some relationships were not working and what he or the individuals needed to do to communicate more effectively in order to resolve their differences. Companies who have sent their employees to LIFO® seminars have discovered that they adopt a **common language** for referring to behavior and performance. This helps to foster discussion and greatly assists the personal review and development process.

- One of the most important characteristics of the method is that it does not suggest in any way that there is only one good style of working and behavior. Each preferred orientation is valuable. There is only a question of difference, not of inequality. There is no threat of being criticized or ridiculed for "what one is." No arbitrary norms are enforced or insisted upon. **This approach emphasizes strategies for leveraging the productive use of different styles for an individual, within teams and in building organizations.**

- With LIFO® concepts you can make a **direct link** between your function, task, work situation, work problems, and cooperation with colleagues and supervisors. This means that the organizational changes and distribution of tasks on the job can be made quickly and effectively.

- Users of LIFO® concepts report that they acquire a depth of information about themselves and how to deal with others that is not available from other methodologies. LIFO® gives us a **blueprint for looking at people** so that things that we observe in others – and, particularly things we observe that bother us about others – are more understandable. Also, as more and more work activity takes place in teams, LIFO® thinking offers a fast and effective way to increase our knowledge about the people who comprise the team. It provides a **mechanism to value and use the strengths of each member of the team.**

CHAPTER 3

THE LIFO® METHOD'S ORIGIN

WHO AM I?

Everybody is in some way searching for who they are during their lifetimes. We all want to understand the "inner me" that gives meaning to who we are and how we behave. Some people get actively involved in this process to learn about themselves through reading, discussions, contemplation, or even various forms of therapy. Other people take a less active, but no less important approach. They consciously or unconsciously pick up information about themselves based on personal experiences or other intellectual and emotional impacts affecting their lives. Some individuals are very keen to understand themselves; others find it an uncomfortable process.

THE IMPORTANCE OF A POSITIVE SELF-CONCEPT

Understanding our self-concepts was a major research interest of Allan Katcher from the earliest days of his career. Among other research, he collaborated with Laura Crowell and S. Frank Miyamoto in studying the relationship of self-concepts to communicative skill. In these studies it became clear that those with favorable self-concepts communicated more and better, and they functioned as leaders more frequently in problem-solving groups. These insights help formulate the basis for the practical elements that drive the LIFO® method.

Katcher's early immersion in group development work with sensitivity training during the 1960's revealed the significant limitations and profound influence of self-esteem on life performance. At about that time the American Management Association had published a study in which high-level executives were interviewed about a number of personal views, including the question "What one thing wouldn't you want your subordinates and superiors to know about you?" Surprisingly, an overwhelming number said, "How inadequate I feel to do the job I have!" Even those who were successful suffered from self-doubts. Katcher wondered about the consequences those feelings had for successful performance of their jobs. Further, it was observed that those who are proud of their achievements and competence often are subject to critical evaluations by others – as if there is something indecent about having a positive attitude about oneself. Conversely, there is evidence that an overly self-critical attitude toward self can precipitate lower performance on the job – perhaps resulting from reluctance to release one's full powers for fear it might be indecent.

One important insight that Katcher gained from sensitivity training was that by recognizing your deepest doubts you do not really change the way others perceive you. After sharing and experiencing intimate thoughts and feelings with others in the group it seemed that the effort one expended to protect others from seeing the "inner self" did more to put them off than to foster understanding, respect and appreciation. The process of learning to view oneself more positively seemed liberating and enhancing.

THE PARADOX OF STRENGTHS AND WEAKNESSES

Later while consulting with several companies on individual performance evaluation Katcher and his partner, Stuart Atkins, experienced some intriguing results. They had developed for these companies a performance review process that involved input from both manager and employee and emphasized performance improvement. At the outset, their experience was that people found it meaningful, fair and useful. Yet, after the first year or so, adherence to the process began to diminish. Perplexed, they interviewed both managers and employees and discovered that neither one was enchanted by the process. The managers felt uncomfortable playing the role of the all-knowing boss and the employees felt anxious about the methodology, despite receiving positive reviews.

Managers would often say, "If I comment about some inadequacy, I run the risk of hurting or angering an otherwise effective employee – I would prefer to evaluate without a discussion!" On the other hand, employees would say, "When I'm told to change some behavior, I feel that if I did I might also change what works best for me." It was as if both sides recognized what Atkins and Katcher discovered after reading Erich Fromm's book, *Man For Himself*: that there is an intimate relationship between productive and ineffective behavior. Indeed, Fromm states, **"Our weaknesses are seldom more than the excessive use of one's strengths."** If this is true, no wonder dissatisfaction is felt with the performance evaluation process. Indeed, this statement is so meaningful to participants in LIFO® seminars that it is often the one thing above all that is remembered about the experience.

STRENGTH MANAGEMENT®

This paradox between our strengths and our weaknesses posed an exciting implication; that is, the path to success depends upon the **management of one's strengths** in the same sense that a business manager achieves results by the way in which he uses resources (personnel, technology, finances and organization). Atkins and Katcher felt that they could make a contribution to the improvement and productivity of relationships by developing a new approach based on this insight. They eventually called it "Strength Management® Strategy."

This concept also aligned with the philosophy of Peter Drucker. In his book *The Practice of Management*, Drucker argued that management is really as much an attitude as a set of techniques – that the "manager" is one who focuses constantly on goals or objectives, commits to continually measuring progress towards goals, and changes or redirects efforts when they fail to achieve desired goals. This concern drives his/her behavior and efforts to influence others.

Such a managerial attitude can be observed in work situations or any life events (e.g. management of health, personal happiness, fortune etc.). Atkins and Katcher felt there was a natural linkage between Drucker's views and those of Fromm. The issue for both was to develop ways in which everyone could optimize the deployment of his or her talents – by managing the ways in which they were used.

UNDERSTANDING AND ACCEPTANCE

There was an additional viewpoint that was influential in the development of the LIFO® approach. This significant impact came from Carl Rogers' perceptive reflections on the essence of the therapeutic, changing, and learning processes. For Rogers, the recognition of the importance of trying to understand and accept another person, communicating that through one's empathetic reflection of what had been revealed, and trusting the other person to work with that acceptance in a positive way seemed crucial to personal change and development.

Consider such statements as these:

"In my relationships with people I have found that it does not help in the long run to act as though I were something that I am not."

"I have found it effective, in my dealings with people, to be accepting of myself."

". . . that we cannot change, we cannot move away from what we are, until we thoroughly accept what we are. Then change seems to come about almost unnoticed."

" I have found it of enormous value when I can permit myself to understand another person. . . . "

These statements represent an outlook and viewpoint that underlie the LIFO® approach. The fact is that such seemingly "simple" attitudes are difficult to achieve – difficult because of our biases, desires for expertise, or even our level of sophistication. We then tend to neglect the importance of empathic understanding in our work. Indeed, in social sciences we are all too often trained to "evaluate" from theoretical frameworks for the sake of "understanding" without realizing the negating effect that has when those evaluations do not match the experience of the person. In performance evaluations at work, this phenomenon results in alienation and the arousal of defensive reactions that work against change.

THE LIFO® METHOD PHILOSOPHY

Atkins and Katcher decided that they wanted the LIFO® method to promote one's awareness of behavioral resources, a sense of uniqueness, an **understanding and *appreciation of the value of one's strengths and those of others*,** and skills in the management of personal and group resources (the combination of Fromm, Rogers and Drucker). They believed that if situations were created to allow each person to make the most of his or her strengths, this would enable everyone to be more effective and more satisfied with work. Further, if a group could leverage such strengths in co-operative recognition, there would be a major productive result from their efforts.

As an initial step, it was necessary to develop an instrument to audit perceived behavior in various situations and to act as a vehicle for self-discovery. This instrument, today known as the LIFO® Survey, would encourage each of us to explore ourselves in a relatively non-defensive and non-threatening way. It would provide us with insights that we could share in a way that would help us interact more satisfactorily with colleagues at work.

Atkins and Katcher, together with Elias Porter, began their efforts by designing the original LIFE® Orientations Survey. It was a way to inventory and recognize the strengths and skills used to cope with successes and failures. They saw this as a powerful tool for discovery and communication, not as a diagnostic instrument. Within the framework of the instrument they also included a subtle, yet valuable way of assessing personal communications congruence (the symmetry of intention, behavior and impact – a unique feature of the LIFO® method). This measurement, in turn, has became the basic LIFO® model for change.

For example, a well-intentioned manager was concerned about the lack of participation in group discussions. His staff consisted of experienced, highly knowledgeable and capable managers. When meetings were videotaped it became evident that the manager's behavior unwittingly contributed to the effect that caused him concern. He would introduce topics by saying, "I would like to share with you how I think such a situation should be handled." Naturally, none of his staff believed he was interested in hearing different opinions. When the manager changed his behavior to simply introduce an issue and invite comments, discussion became vigorous. By understanding his own *intentions* (desire to have participation), watching his own *behavior* (videotaping) and observing the *impact* (no participation), he realized he needed to change his approach.

As Atkins and Katcher examined relationships between orientation patterns and a variety of behavioral areas (communicating, leading, decision making, planning, negotiating, team participation, etc.) they began to realize that there were many layers of depth involved in understanding the forces involved. The key principles of the LIFO® method were born.

KEY PRINCIPLES OF THE LIFO® METHOD

REVISING THE "GOLDEN RULE"

All of us are aware of the "Golden Rule." Treat others the way *we* would like to be treated. This basic view on life is important and has been espoused across most religions. For example, consider the following:

> Tse-kung asked, "Is there one word which may serve as a rule of practice for all one's life?" The Master said, "Is not Reciprocity such a word? What you do not want done to yourself, do not to others."
> —Confucius (551-479 B.C.E.), Chinese philosopher, founder of Confucianism in the *Analects*

> No man is a true believer unless he desireth for his brother that which he desireth for himself.
> —Muhammad (570-632 C.E.), prophet of Islam

> Whatsoever you would that men should not do to you, do not do that to them. This is the whole law. The rest is only explanation.
> —Hillel Ha-Babli in the Talmud c. 50 B.C.E.

> As ye would that men should do to you, do ye also to them likewise.
> —Luke 6:31, c. 75 C.E.

The LIFO® Golden Rule, a phrase that underpins the LIFO® method, takes a different slant on this. LIFO® thinking says:

Treat others the way *they* would like to be treated.

MANAGING BY KNOWING OTHERS

To be effective one must know about others – understand their needs, concerns perceptions and values and act accordingly. A gift you might like, for example, may mean nothing to someone who has different interests. A compliment which you deem to be high praise may fall on deaf ears to someone who needs to feel specially recognized for what they value. Criticism that you feel would be helpful might be experienced as a devastating evaluation by an employee.

MANAGING THROUGH UNDERSTANDING AND ACCEPTANCE

Reorienting our attitudes toward others, as described in the work of Carl Rogers, requires a willingness to suspend judgment, to forego giving advice, instead expending effort to listen to what other people are feeling and thinking, to discover how they see their world and the events affecting them. The LIFO® Method will provide some frameworks for understanding other people, accepting them and appreciating their strengths. In turn such knowledge helps you to manage your strengths in that you learn to use the strengths of others.

LIFO® VALUES

The LIFO® method is more than a technique; it is *a **way of thinking***. Other methodologies exist that will allow an individual to do self-examination in order to determine his or her so-called personality type. However, most stop at that point. LIFO® thinking carries beyond that to assist us in *changing* **our behavior** in order to work with others more effectively.

Furthermore, LIFO® thinking suggests every person has a broader *repertoire of behaviors* than he/she typically demonstrates or maybe even realizes. LIFO® approaches attempt to help us unleash this power that is within us all.

LIFO® thinking recognizes that changing one's behavior is not easy. It is not just a question of doing it or not doing it, rather it is a question of *first consciously understanding what one prefers to do*. Learning about how and why we prefer to behave in certain ways is explicit in the LIFO® process. From there we can explore why certain behaviors have been used in various situations and whether they have been the most appropriate ones to employ.

The LIFO® approach is *non-judgmental.* It starts from the premise that any of us can change in any situation if we know how to manage ourselves. And because it is non-valuing it is *meaningful and valid in multi-cultural situations.*

LIFO® thinking does not propose that there is an ideal type or configuration for a manager, a leader, a spouse, etc. In fact, LIFO® concepts support the idea that there are *many ways to be successful* that are not tied to being a particular type. Furthermore, LIFO® thinking does **not assume that your behavior is consistent across all situations.** It does not agree that once you identify certain personal skills, those and only those are what you have to work with.

CHAPTER 4

THE STRENGTH MANAGEMENT PARADOX

Every now and then you come across a statement that really makes you sit up and pay attention, something that offers you a glimpse of a fundamental truth that you sort of knew but had not quite captured until you saw it in print. Such was the case with Stuart Atkins *and* Allan Katcher when *they* read Eric Fromm's statement in *Man For Himself*:

"A man's weakness is seldom more than the excessive use of his strengths."

Just think of the implications of this statement. If your weaknesses are the result of overusing your strengths, to improve your effectiveness with people you only have to reduce the frequency and maybe also intensity of the strengths that you use. Of course, this is possible if first, you could recognize how you are using your strengths *and* then understand their effects on others. You do not really have to change yourself, but rather you must learn to manage the attributes you already possess. For example, you feel you get a lot of things done because you are able to respond quickly to events. However, you have found that at times making quick decisions can backfire. Your somewhat impulsive behavior meant that you failed to consider some very important facts. While you may not want to develop yourself into a cautious and deliberate thinker, learning to slow down a bit to deal with certain circumstances is within your grasp. In fact, you may be able

---

to see an easy way to curb this excess; that is, you can use the strengths of others on your team who are more reflective to provide you with some ideas or other viewpoints for consideration before you act. We call this strength management strategy "extending." More about that later.

Thus, a whole new approach suggests itself: **strength management as a path to effective behavior.**

YIN AND YANG

People living in Western societies tend to think quite separately about their strengths and their weaknesses, to treat the former as good and the latter as bad. Yet in Far Eastern cultures the concept of yin and yang would suggest something different. Such a concept suggest that each thing contains both elements. Indeed, typical Western training methodologies are focused on ways to overcome weaknesses rather than as opportunities to use effectively one's strengths. They also tend to advocate the need for people to change others, instead of accepting people as they are and finding the best way to function given their available strengths.

Many people are truly burdened by their weaknesses. In one of our recent seminars a manager said, "Don't tell me about my strengths, tell me about my weaknesses and what I can do to get rid of them." Most of you know where that often leads during a discussion. The person tightens up to prepare for the worst and becomes highly defensive when you present your criticisms. Performance evaluations are usually anxious affairs precisely because people feel the negative things will be emphasized and the positive ones ignored.

STRENGTHS AND WEAKNESSES:

YOU CAN'T HAVE ONE WITHOUT THE OTHER!

Yet, surprisingly your "bad" points could not even be cited unless the "good" ones were also there. Someone could not demonstrate **arrogance,** for example, unless they already possessed a fair amount of **self-confidence. Procrastination** would not be so common unless those practicing it brought a positive sense of **cautiousness** to their tasks. While we like to see employees who are **trying to be responsive to others,** if they do it too much that can appear to be **overly submissive.** Even the desirable trait of **flexibility** could be exhibited as **aimlessness** when overdone.

Here are a few other examples of productive use of strengths and what may be considered unproductive use if those strengths if used too much or maybe used at the wrong time depending on a situation.

PRODUCTIVE USE	EXCESSIVE USE
If you use your strength effectively you are seen as...	*If you use your strength too much or in an inappropriate situation you may sometimes be seen as...*
Considerate	Self-denying
Trusting	Gullible
Responsive	Over-committed
Directing	Domineering
Self-confident	Arrogant
Competitive	Antagonistic
Practical	Unimaginative
Firm	Stubborn
Prudent	Cautious
Flexible	Inconsistent
Adaptable	Compliant
Humorous	Frivolous

OUR EXCESSES ARE THE CULPRITS

Ironically enough, it is therefore the "too much of a good thing" that gives us problems. We develop skill and talent as a result of being able to achieve success with our behaviors and therefore we tend to use those behaviors as much as we can – sometimes too much. It is quite natural to rely on those approaches that have worked for us before.

Consider the case of an employee known for his decisiveness and ability to take charge. He gets appointed to a major management post. Within a short time after he becomes a manager, morale among employees in his group deteriorates, especially among the supervisors. Looking more closely, we see that our new manager tries to do everything by himself, has little patience for the efforts of others, and seldom allows others, even knowledgeable experts, to participate in any decision-making. What is happening here? A chat with the new manager reveals his perception that since he felt his promotion was due to his assertiveness and initiative he assumed that he would be expected to demonstrate those qualities in the new position, perhaps even more than he had before.

What is attractive to us at first encounter may become offensive upon too frequent exposure. Even charming conversation, when overdone, can cause others to turn off if the charmer does not allow them to speak as well. A sensitive employee asked to reply to questions from an aggressive manager may be made to feel as if he's engaged more in combat than a business discussion. This can truly alter the quality of the answers that he provides. Among salespeople, the term "bought it back" refers to someone who lost a sale because he did not know when to stop selling when the sale had already been made. Even at home a devoted parent can antagonize a child through over-protective behavior, despite good and kindly intentions. The impact is far beyond what was expected.

TRYING TOO HARD

Many people believe if you run into difficulties, all you need to do is try harder to achieve success. Yet, there are instances of team performance, as in sports, where the team falls behind; each member tries his utmost to perform, only to find that as the harder each team member tries, the worse the team's performance becomes. One can try too hard – the excess of the trying is the problem. Sometimes using less of a behavior can produce more effective results.

TWO REASONS FOR OUR EXCESSES

If excessive behavior has such undesirable consequences, why do we do it? First of all we may not even recognize that the behavior is excessive. If you find people listening and laughing at my jokes, it is quite natural for you to persist until the laughter ceases.

The first cause is the **rewarding aspect of the behavior** itself. You keep doing something because it is satisfying to do so – you believe it is having a productive consequence, favoring your interests and maybe enhancing your reputation. Previous experience may also make you believe that this is how it works. You simply fail to notice how your excessive behavior is affecting others or the task to be done.

In some circumstances however, **the threatening character of the situation** creates a high degree of tension. Facing threatening situations – such as risking the loss of status or resources – can trigger responses that are far out of proportion to the situation, often without your even being aware. In the earlier example of an aggressive manager questioning a sensitive employee, the employee may have replied weakly because the questioning was perceived as challenging, perhaps questioning the value of a previous statement the employee had made. The employee may not have felt sure about the statement in the first place – or the questioner was someone whose authority was higher than that of the person being questioned. We may not know why a person is being threatened but the presence of excessive behavior tells us that a threat is indeed present (even if logically, it should not be).

Fortunately, there are several ways to control excesses that will be discussed in a later chapter. First, however, we have to understand what we do, how we do it and what are the effects of our behavioral patterns.

CHAPTER 5

AN INTRODUCTION TO LIFO®
STYLES

OUR UNIQUENESS

There's something special about you – your different way of feeling and thinking, your way of speaking, your distinctive set of habits, your unique experiences – something that marks your identity. The uniqueness we all possess means that when presented with a new opportunity we deal with it in different ways. Some people just jump in and try to take advantage of a new situation. Others want to study it carefully, weigh the benefits and risks before doing anything. Still others will look to how others are reacting before joining in. If we step back and observe how people make decisions, not only in this case but also in other aspects of life, we would discover patterns. We often hear people say things like, "Isn't that just like him!" or "You'd just know it was him!" These statements reflect the particular patterns that characterize a person.

We start life with differences. One baby cries a lot, another seems calm most of the time; one smiles when spoken to, another does not. A sensitive baby responds irritably to any change, while another seems placid. Your family provided circumstances and experiences that built on these differences. These made you different and more unique. You received rewards for doing things certain ways and punishments for ones that met with disapproval. You learned it was easy to do some things, hard to do others. As a result you began to learn that success was achieved in certain ways, acceptance occurred by espousing some values and not others. You became *YOU*. You found it easy to learn or like some subjects and hate others. As life went on, the marks of events and influence of individuals further moulded and shaped the person you are. Think back to family, friends, teachers, achievements and failures.

Your behavior is not really random. Watch someone carefully and you will observe patterns in their actions. All of us exhibit habits of choice, time management, the organization of material and events, decision-making styles, a particular manner of asking questions, a way of relating to our bosses, colleagues, friends, spouses and children. In short, the major dimensions of life seem to reflect patterned preferences of behavior.

LIFE ORIENTATIONS®

The organization of goals, values, attitudes and behaviors that seem to be related to a common theme are called **Life Orientations®** in the LIFO® system.

To be sure, the pattern is not always uniform, although within a certain range of situations certain common elements seem to be emphasized repeatedly. Thus, even though you might be highly organized while engaged in a hobby like collecting stamps, your overall behavior might be highly spontaneous and not very organized at all. A preference for dealing with situations without plans, without efforts to keep track of what has happened – repeated in many situations – this would be indicative of the presence of a fundamental orientation.

There may be tremendous value for you in using this spontaneous **style of behavior** (the word style is used interchangeably with **orientation**). You might be able to use intuitive thinking in any situation. You might not need a great deal of direction. You might feel free to deviate from policies and procedures without discomfort. In turn, you are likely to value such beliefs as "I feel that one should not be bound by rules," or, "I think one should be open to all that life provides and use my energies accordingly, rather than wasting time on orderliness and organization."

UNDERSTANDING YOUR OWN STRENGTHS

Before we get into a description of the LIFO® orientations, it is useful to first take a moment to reflect on your own style. This will help you obtain a fuller appreciation of your own orientation patterns and their origins. Answer the following questions:

1. What do you think are your major strengths (talents, skills, and achievements – your "claim to fame")? What do you do well?
2. What would others say are your most distinctive characteristics?
3. How do situations at work provide opportunities for you to use your strengths?
4. What are the characteristics you admire most in others?
5. What are some of the things you do that have a negative impact on your productivity and relationships (behaviors you would like to modify)?
6. When you are in conflict with someone, how are you likely to react?
7. How do you behave when under pressure or stress?

Were these questions easy to answer? Many people find it hard to list their strengths, at least with full objectivity. You may be a little hesitant to brag about yourself. You may even tend to discount or fail to appreciate fully your own talents and skills. After someone has accomplished something distinctive you might hear him or her say, "Oh anybody can do that, that's nothing special!" On the other hand you may have noticed that most folks who are technically capable and also have a healthy dose of self-confidence are much less hesitant to mention their assets to others.

ACKNOWLEDGING YOUR OWN VALUE

It's important to appreciate yourself and at the same time it's also important to value others, even those who do things differently or who think differently. We need to learn to celebrate the differences in points of view as a source of new thinking and stimulation for ourselves, particularly as an aid when functioning as a team. What did you reply for Question 3? Do you value only people whose characteristics are similar to your own? Think also about the times you get into trouble in your relationships (Question 4). Have you, for example, overdone a behavior when you have been under pressure and strain? Why does this happen? Did you resolve the situation successfully? The descriptions of the LIFO® orientations will give you some clear ideas about why conflicts can occur and later in this book, what you can do to remedy difficult situations.

THE FOUR BASIC ORIENTATIONS

While there are many orientations, **four major patterns** seem to underlie and relate to the dominant phases of our lives. In the LIFO® method these four styles are built from our understanding of four key underlying needs every individual possesses in varying degrees:

UNDERLYING NEEDS

To make a valuable contribution
To set and achieve goals
To minimize damage and loss
To enjoy harmony and social acceptability

Think about it. Every one of our actions in some way falls within these personal, very human needs.

Let's take a closer look at our individual **preoccupations and concerns**. Consider the following chart. The vertical axis reflects a continuum of concern that is commonly seen in people's behavior on the job. Some people are more concerned about *how people are affected* (at the top of the axis) while other people have a primary preoccupation with *getting the task accomplished* (towards the bottom of the axis). The horizontal axis represents the fact that there are people who measure all or most of their behaviors using themselves as the key reference point, i.e. *self-referenced*, concerned about how events affect themselves (at the left of the axis). Others tend to relate their behaviors to how they relate beyond their own needs and desires i.e. *other-referenced*.

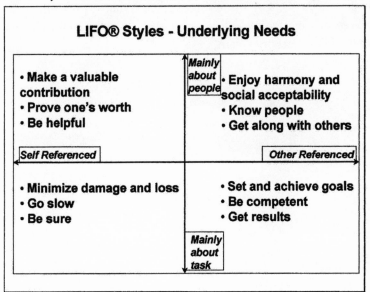

Taking this analysis one step further we can describe each of these four underlying needs with one word that sums up the key **drivers** behind those behaviors.

UNDERLYING NEEDS	KEY BEHAVIORAL DRIVERS
To make a valuable contribution	IDEALS or EXCELLENCE
To set and achieve goals	ACTION
To minimize damage and loss	REASON
To enjoy harmony and social acceptability	HARMONY

READING OTHER PEOPLE'S "NEEDS"

Take a moment to see if you can recognize someone's underlying needs simply by listening to what they say or how they express themselves. Here is a list of ten statements. In the appropriate column at the right put a check mark in the box corresponding to the key driver you feel is being expressed. Some statements may represent a combination of two drivers. The answers follow after the chart.

	IDEALS	ACTION	REASON	HARMONY
1. Tell me what needs my attention, otherwise don't report.				
2. I like people to check with me before they take action.				
3. Good will and feelings are more important to me than who is right.				
4. I do what is required, get things accomplished, and keep matters to myself.				
5. I like to consult with colleagues to see what the best decision is before acting.				
6. As long as a person produces, she stays in my favor.				
7. A decision isn't made until I make sure all are agreeable to it.				
8. I require specific information to keep abreast of things.				
9. I act decisively, but like to keep people informed about what I'm thinking.				
10. I like to persuade other people to do what I think is best.				

Answers:

1. Action
2. Reason
3. Harmony
4. Reason
5. Ideals

6. Action
7. Harmony
8. Ideals
9. Action with Harmony
10. Action with Ideals

43

You will have noted that questions 9 and 10 correspond to a combination of two needs. Since people are not simple organisms we are sometimes driven by more than one need at the same time. More often than not one of our needs is stronger than the other, but it is possible that they are equally forceful in affecting how we behave. It is also conceivable that there may even be a third need that mixes with the two others.

To summarize, the four underlying needs are the basis for the four styles used in the LIFO® method. Dealing with only four orientations makes the understanding of people's behavior easy to describe and talk about. We will see that this does not in any way hinder the depth to which you can go in analysing your own and others' behaviors. In the LIFO® approach, the four drivers have been given names that reflect the strengths that characterizes typical behaviors resulting from those underlying needs. The names of the four styles used and the key drivers they represent are as follows:

LIFO® STYLES	DRIVEN BY...
Supporting-Giving	IDEALS
Controlling-Taking	ACTION
Conserving-Holding	ANALYSIS
Adapting-Dealing	HARMONY

It is important to emphasize that unlike terms used in other behavioral or personality analysis methodologies we are **not talking about** *types*. These four style names represent patterns of behaviors that you may exhibit given your personality and how you act in a specific situation. This is why they are designated with the ending **"ing."** These are not labels of type; instead they are descriptions of behavior, **the strengths we use to affect outcomes.** These orientations are fully described in the next chapters. But before we get there, let's discuss the importance of these situations in which we use our various behaviors.

STYLES AND WORKING CONDITIONS

We have used the term "style" to refer to the patterns of behavior used by people to satisfy their needs. These styles influence how you deal with situations when things are going well *and* also when you are experiencing frustration, conflict and stress.

It would be ideal if in our work or personal lives we only encountered situations in which we feel high levels of comfort. In LIFO® terms we refer to these situations as **Favorable Conditions.** These occur when things are going well for us. We have the resources we need, we are familiar with the situation and we have coped well with similar situations in the past.

But life and work life in particular are not like that. More and more often we are being pushed to operate "outside of our comfort zone." In LIFO® terms we call these **Unfavorable or Adverse Conditions.** In these situations things may be rough. Circumstances and people frustrate us, we lack support, we are threatened, and we experience risk or conflict.

Sometimes we behave the same in both conditions, favorable and unfavorable. Many of us do not, however. When there is a difference between the favorable and unfavorable patterns it is caused by our life experiences. When both parents exhibit the same styles we are more likely to learn consistent ways to approach all situations. However, when parental orientations are very different, the exact influence on a child's behavior may vary, depending upon the quality of the relationship, the consistency and amount of reward and punishment provided, and the parent (or surrogate) who is the most frequent source of discipline. A parent may emphasize acting boldly when things go well but recommend caution when they do not.

Now it should be clearer why using the same behavior in different situations may be inappropriate for getting results or why using a behavior to excess may lead to problems. Do you recall the table in an earlier chapter that showed descriptions of productive use of strengths and how they might be perceived if used to excess? Once again here is that table, only this time we have added more strengths and we have also included the name of the LIFO® styles that are indicative of those strengths. By looking at each strength and word to describe the excessive use of that strength you will also get a sense of how the LIFO® style names were developed.

PRODUCTIVE USE	EXCESSIVE USE
If you use your strength effectively you are seen as...	*If you use your strength too much or in an inappropriate situation you may sometimes be seen as...*
SUPPORTING	**GIVING**
Considerate	Self-denying
Trusting	Gullible
Responsive	Over-committed
Seeks Improvement	Perfectionist
Modest	Self-effacing
CONTROLLING	**TAKING**
Directing	Domineering
Self-confident	Arrogant
Competitive	Antagonistic
Quick to Act	Impulsive
CONSERVING	**HOLDING**
Practical	Unimaginative
Firm	Stubborn
Prudent	Cautious
Reserved	Uncommunicative
Thorough	Pedantic

ADAPTING	DEALING
Flexible	Inconsistent
Adaptable	Compliant
Humorous	Frivolous
Empathetic	Insincere
Resourceful	Tricky

The differences between the productive words in the left-hand column and their related excessive use descriptions in the right-hand column are rather striking. It is interesting to note how very desirable behaviors can be linked to undesirable ones – an example of the strength-weakness paradox discussed in the last chapter. Indeed, after sitting in on many performance and promotion review discussions over the years, it was fascinating to note how both of these aspects of a person's behavior were revealed in the discussions. This is testimony to the interconnectedness of strengths and weaknesses.

UNIVERSAL CHARACTERISTICS OF THE LIFO® METHOD

To summarize, here are eight key characteristics of the LIFO® method that are important to understand before you dive deeper into your own behavioral style and try to understand those of others.

1. All individuals are influenced by all four LIFO® orientations. The exact mix and our individual ability to execute those behaviors is what create our uniqueness.
2. Orientations can be described in terms of influences or reactions to favorable or unfavorable conditions.
3. Orientations can influence behavior to be productive or excessive depending upon the frequency, intensity and appropriateness for a situation.

4. There is no "ideal" orientation. This varies depending upon the group, situation and culture.

5. No research exists that demonstrates any particular orientation is healthier, more successful or better than any other.

6. There is an enormous overlap in the use of orientations, even though statistics might point to some differences between groups and classes of people. For example, women in the United States seem to use more "Supporting-Giving" behaviors than men (as do Japanese men), but there is an extensive amount of overlap – so much so that you could not recognize any particular group membership because a style was used.

7. Your background, experiences and training determine your own orientation pattern. Like any well-established habit (in this case, set of habits), it is difficult to change. If you ever tried to stop smoking or change your eating habits you would readily discover the terrible tyranny of a habit. In the case of orientation patterns they are not only resistant to change because they are habitual, but because they are highly functional and have proven successful and satisfying to you. During your lifetime you have a natural need to preserve your sense of identity. This is a source of power – your strength.

8. Some aspects of your behavior can be changed. This entails a disciplined effort to control the behavior and attitudes, redirect them and then initiate new responses to the same situations. The effects can be altered, for example, by modifying the intensities of your behavior ("You don't have to get *so* angry!"). Or you may eliminate the presence of some behavior by changing your understanding of a situation (a sailboat heeling may not mean disaster, but just a natural

response to wind, or an airplane bouncing in the sky is like a car on a bumpy road). A question may no longer evoke impatience and irritation because you have learned to recognize and value someone's need for clarity and structure. To be able to make these changes, you need to know your own mix of orientations and then make a deliberate effort to change.

In the orientation descriptions that follow, we have deliberately exaggerated some features to make it easier to learn about them. There is some danger in this procedure in that it may encourage you to think in "stereotypes." These descriptions, however, only illustrate. They do not define the style any more than the title of a style does. For example, a person who is described as demonstrating a high amount of Supporting-Giving behavior does not *necessarily* exhibit all of the orientation description for Supporting-Giving listed in the tables included in this book.

To complicate matters, the orientations are influenced by each other. You may have observed some leaders who work in similar ways, but have different impacts on people and results. Thus, two managers can be forceful and directive. One relies primarily on careful planning, clearly defined responsibilities, and meticulous review of performance. The other is equally forceful but relies more on personal relationships, mutual objective setting, and delegation of responsibility. Both can accomplish a great deal. Each pattern will be seen as favorable by some and not by others. As a matter of fact, **there is no uniformly effective and favorable leadership pattern.**

SUMMARIZING THE LIFO® STRENGTH MANAGEMENT FUNDAMENTALS

- We learn to behave towards each other in ways that seem best to satisfy our different psychological and physical needs for self-fulfilment. This behavior becomes our natural or "preferred" orientation towards other people.

- This preferred orientation represents the source of our strengths which – when we are able to understand, develop and manage them – can be even more productive in satisfying our needs.

- The combination of behavioral orientations that make up our behavioral style is not, however, infallible in satisfying needs. When our strengths are carried to excess they can be counterproductive; they become, in fact, our weaknesses.

- This tendency for our strengths to be used in excess becomes most counter-productive as our environment is affected by conditions of stress and of conflict. Through the LIFO® Method we can unlock ourselves from styles of behavior that frustrate our basic goal of self-fulfilment and provide options for managing situations.

In the next four chapters we will describe those who emphasize a particular orientation as if they were a type. This is only done to help you understand the differences between them. We all use all of the orientations. The dominant pattern is what others will readily recognize about us.

CHAPTER 6

THE
SUPPORTING-GIVING
ORIENTATION (SG)

The LIFO® Styles		
SUPPORTING/ GIVING	*Mainly about people*	
		ADAPTING/DEALING
Self Referenced		*Other Referenced*
CONSERVING/HOLDING		CONTROLLING/TAKING
	Mainly about task	

Koyo Tamashiro

A SUPPORTING-GIVING CASE STUDY

Koyo Tamashiro supervises the research and development group of a major Japanese electronics firm. An amiable person, he seems to be a pleasant although somewhat shy person. His group contains a number of brilliant and resourceful engineers, some of whom have gone on to key positions in other corporate decisions. Koyo is a good teacher and developer of people. New personnel are often assigned to his group for the thorough training they can receive under his direction. He provides many opportunities for participation in decision-making meetings. Information sharing is encouraged and a fair amount of freedom is provided individuals in executing assignments.

Koyo's initial kindness is sometimes offset by a quiet and critical manner when he reviews others' work. He is always ready to provide advice or guidance when requested but tends to leave people alone if they don't. He expects people to keep him informed regularly about progress but won't demand reports. When he receives reports he reviews them conscientiously and redlines comments all over the report. It is difficult to get an unqualified approval and acknowledgment unless the report is free of errors. One can easily get the impression that he is never satisfied. Despite such behavior he is supportive of his people and will recommend them highly to others. When one scientist expressed surprise about his overall ranking considering all of the critical remarks that Koyo had made about his work, Koyo replied, "If I hadn't thought so well of you, I would never have spent the time on criticism. I did that because I wanted to help you develop into a better scientist than you were."

His staff believes he is not comfortable in dealing with higher levels of management. He doesn't seem to argue strongly enough to make sure the group gets what it needs. Koyo seems to rely too much on the goodwill and understanding of others and is not willing to confront issues forcefully enough, or fight in a confident and determined way for what he wants. In fact, during a major reduction in funds, his group received more than their share of the "bad news." Yet there are some times when a principle is at stake that Koyo really fights hard and generally wins his case. This happened when Production unfairly blamed Research for an inept design when it was really the fault of the Quality control department.

Koyo is also inclined to take promises for granted. He was recently told that a new laboratory had been authorized and patiently waited for construction to begin. It didn't happen for seven months. When discussing the issue he would express dissatisfaction but never lodged a formal complaint.

Koyo is as hard on himself as anyone else is. A modest man, despite his high capability he blames himself if anything goes wrong.

He is strongly devoted to his family and tries to spend as much time as he can with his children, despite a very heavy work schedule. Koyo and his wife are very concerned about their children's education, emphasize the value of studying, and celebrate achievements.

Family Background

Koyo was the second child in a family of five. The family was moderately prosperous and owned several stores. The father and mother knew each other from childhood and were married in their late teens. While the family's financial status steadily progressed, their lifestyle remained fairly constant. Throughout Koyo's childhood and adolescence the family lived in the same house. The father regretted that he had not gone to college and insisted that all of his children seriously prepare themselves for higher education. Schoolwork was expected to be completed before they were allowed to play. Since Koyo was very bright, he received a lot of praise from his parents.

The family table talk reviewed school progress and important events. Family decisions were made by the parents – often the mother. Although authoritatively disposed, the parents were considerate and concerned about feelings. His father could be an impatient man, albeit well intentioned. Koyo remembers that one day when helping his father to replace a windowpane, he dropped a hammer and broke the new glass. The father, furious, called him "the clumsiest person in the whole country!" Koyo states that he never forgot that and as a result he resolved to learn how to fix things so there would never be another mistake. While the father did things with Koyo and his brothers, Koyo always felt a little uneasy with him. It was easier for him to talk with his mother, who shared an avid interest in music and provided a lot of encouragement for his model building by exhibiting them when completed. He felt both parents provided a lot of support but were excessively restrictive during his adolescence.

Koyo couldn't recall receiving any physical punishment from his parents but he dreaded their reactions to school progress or misbehavior. When he did not perform at his very best, his parents made him feel that he had disappointed them. As a result, despite emerging as the third highest student in school, he felt he hadn't really learned as much as he could because he was so anxious about succeeding. He found he learned best when taught by people who were truly expert and yet encouraged questions and different approaches. While at Tokyo University, he was so inspired by one of his physics professors that he decided to pursue a scientific career.

As a result of some outstanding doctoral research, he was hired by his current company 15 years ago. He feels he has been well treated by the company and that he would like to stay with them until he retires. Changing conditions in Japan have led to offers from other companies, but he has turned them down.

He is generally contented with his life, desirous of improving his knowledge and seeing possibilities for new research realized through the dedicated work of his colleagues and himself. He feels the quality of life, the opportunity to exercise his skills and knowledge and the chance to stay close to his family and friends are the things that provide value for him.

Supporting-Giving Characteristics in Comfortable Situations

If this orientation characterized your predominant behavior you would be someone who wants to be respected while being seen as a **"good person."** SGs like being nice to people and doing their share to make a contribution. Interested in **maintaining ideals and values,** SGs strongly believe that each of us can help make this a better world to live in. Thus what is of greatest concern to SGs is having a **sense of mission and purpose,** behaving in such a way that they feel they are living up to their best intentions and capabilities.

Key to their efforts is the **importance of not simply preaching but doing** – serving as an example for others, trying to be responsive and cooperative. Behaving in this way gives SGs an inner sense of satisfaction that goes beyond receiving external recognition.

SGs tend to be **modest** – not boasting about personal behavior or requesting recognition, although they do feel good when others acknowledge and appreciate their personal efforts.

SGs are willing to **believe in the worth and value of others** and are interested in **helping people grow and develop**.

When they become members of a group SGs like to be able to **share its goals and values.** Once this is understood they are dedicated to enhancing the team's welfare, expecting appropriate guidance and direction from leaders, preferably people who have personal integrity and have earned respect through their competence.

SGs believe that **rewards will come from being earned** – that a "good deed" will bring its just desserts. Ideals serve as standards. Thus they are always comparing themselves and others to those standards, hopefully meeting them through constant striving for improvement. Failure to meet such goals often leads SGs to feelings of disappointment, disillusionment and guilt.

Supporting-Giving Characteristics in Conflict and Crisis Situations

In situations where **conflict** is present an SG will display a desire to deal with the other person in a **fair and reasonable** way with the expectation that there will be reciprocity.

SGs have little interest in trying to take advantage of the other person and **great distaste and discomfort for emotional confrontations**. Often, they find it difficult to directly ask for something they want or expect, hoping the other person recognizes the need and then gratifies it.

When pressed hard, the SG will likely **accede** to the other person, without expressing reservations. Thus others will often feel that it is **easy to get along with the SG.** All too often SGs tend to **feel overly responsible** for getting a task done or even for the behavior of the group.

Supporting-Giving Assets

- Striving for excellence
- Listening to what people have to say
- Appreciating others' abilities to solve problems
- Providing resources necessary for others to get things done
- Encouraging others when they meet difficulties
- Anticipating the needs of another person and taking care of them in advance
- Cooperating and collaborating with others to expedite a task, make it easier, more enjoyable, etc.
- Lending a hand
- Removing roadblocks that may be in someone's way
- Preparing the way for someone
- Being considerate of another person's time or difficulties and not intruding with your own needs, demands, or burdening the person with additional inputs

- Providing the value of one's experience and advice to facilitate progress (if requested)
- Undertaking an assignment in a willing, wholehearted and dedicated manner
- Trusting others

An Important Note about the SG Orientation

Many people seize on the term "excellence" that is so closely identified with the Supporting-Giving orientation. It is a term used to provide an easy feature to remember and it may provide an inaccurate tone. It is not that "SGs" are driven by excellence per se as much as they feel they have to live up to some standard that is always better than they can achieve – as if there is no way they can satisfy the expectations they perhaps may have internalized from their parents. This does not mean that they behave excellently (indeed there are "Conserving-Holdings" who are more consistent in this regard, especially when it involves living according to a code).

The underlying sense is not that of, for example, practicing and developing skills to be used with confidence, as much as operating from a deep sense of guilt for not being what one believes one should be (or what one's parents felt they should be). Thus one of the problems faced by those who emphasize this orientation is that they do not trust their own standards, do not fully appreciate who they are and value themselves positively. They concentrate more on what they are not, what they lack and feel all too apologetic for their excesses, almost as if they didn't really own them.

To understand this orientation – as all orientations – fully, you should focus more on the underlying goals and philosophy. You should not attend only to the behavior itself but review the behavior in terms of the underlying driving forces. Thus, sometimes behavior that looks like another style might really be "SG" if one understands the intention.

CHAPTER 7

THE CONTROLLING-TAKING ORIENTATION (CT)

The LIFO® Styles	
SUPPORTING/GIVING	ADAPTING/DEALING
CONSERVING/HOLDING	**CONTROLLING/ TAKING**

Mainly about people — *Self Referenced* / *Other Referenced* — *Mainly about task*

Bob James

A CONTROLLING-TAKING CASE STUDY

Bob James has always been an outgoing person starting from his earliest days growing up in the suburbs of a major city in the Northeast of the United States. Today Bob co-manages a private equity investment firm that he started with two partners over ten years ago. Before that Bob had worked his way up the corporate ladder as a banker in three different financial institutions.

Bob's style is dynamic and enthusiastic no matter what endeavour he chooses. He enjoys work most when he is challenged and involved in new and difficult tasks. Achievement, a fast and busy pace, and working with friendly and cooperative people are highly satisfying to him. Bob has always believed that given dedicated energy and imagination – and if in his area of expertise and experience – any problem can be solved through his own personal involvement.

While Bob understands that rules and processes are important, he appreciates it most when he can get and give quick go-aheads to projects. He enjoys a stimulating argument on proposals and looks for his colleagues to actively debate issues, but not for too long. He believes that performance should be measured by results and rewarded accordingly.

Anyone who knows Bob can readily see that recognition and reputation are important to him. But at the same time he will work hard as a team player if he sees that others are working enthusiastically on the problem or project with him. In meetings he shows enthusiasm for issues and expects others to get excited as well.

Bob's inclinations are diverse and include seeing new opportunities or creating them on his own, searching out what he needs to learn and finding ways to learn quickly, recognising obstacles without being stumped by them, starting and leading new projects, putting ideas into effect, being influential, and convincing others of his ideas and/or to work with him.

Bob's co-workers admire his energy and drive, although sometimes they think he is trying to accomplish too much at the same time. When this happens he can find it difficult to keep track of all the pertinent details and manage the processes without their assistance. Generally, as a manager, Bob emphasizes performance, achievement and results. At the same time he takes an interest in his people to ensure they achieve their mission. When goals are set he will demonstrate commitment and persistence in achieving them. He expects the same of others. Once someone proves they are capable, Bob is willing to entrust them with important matters and responsibilities, expecting them to function at high levels with professionalism and a minimum of direction.

Bob sees time as something to manage. He experiences most matters as urgent. Tasks are to be completely quickly and deadlines met.

His direct style means that his colleagues can get clear decisions when needed. They also find that he will confront disagreement directly in an attempt to clear the air. In confrontation he will state his view and actively protect his rights and interests. Bob tends to persist on most issues important to him until a clearcut resolution is achieved.

When he is asked to consider any sort of change, Bob's initial reaction is positive, especially if it will lead to support of his own interests. If going forward with a change is agreed upon, he will play his part with a sense of initiative and energy to achieve the revised course of action. When obstacles are encountered or he is under stress, he will push even harder to get results. His vigorous approach may alienate some colleagues and at these times he can make heavy support demands on others. At the same time he, himself, can lose focus.

Outside the office Bob is equally driven by achievement. Ever since schoolboy days he has been involved in competitive sports. Today he mainly plays tennis and golf, but sees both of these activities as a means to challenge opponents and himself to perform better. He is active in several volunteer organizations where his experience has been used to raise funds. Bob goes after these assignments with zeal and energy. His success and subsequent heightened stature in the community are side effects that give him great pride.

Bob is married and has two children, both now attending private secondary school. His wife practiced as a speech therapist at a major hospital, but no longer does so, as she spends much of her time arranging the family's complicated daily schedules. She, however, is also active as a volunteer in her children's school.

Family Background

Bob is the eldest son of a family of two brothers and one sister. His father owned a successful hardware store in a big city and later expanded it into a chain of stores that covered the East Coast. The mother had graduated from high school and worked as a bookkeeper when she met the father at a church picnic. A whirlwind courtship ensued and Bob was born two years after they were married. A grandfather who had been a Colonel in WWI and involved in politics for a number of years also lived with the James family.

Bob was an only child for five years, after which his siblings were born, spaced approximately two years apart. His oldest sibling was a sister with whom he had and still does have an excellent relationship. Because of the age difference, he never became close to his brothers although their relationship improved after Bob married. His parents and grandfather doted on him, encouraged him to try all kinds of things but insisted he always finish what he started. Chores were assigned to all of the children and they were expected to finish them. If not done properly, they had to keep working until they satisfied the parents and grandfather. Bob had a strong bond to his grandfather who regaled him with all kinds of tales about his military and political experience. He emphasized the importance of achieving, and the value of being prepared and confident in order to achieve success. The general theme was "You can do it!" Good effort was not viewed as enough – you had to accomplish what you had started out to do.

Bob's parents provided lots of freedom but also firm limits. While they didn't ask him to account for his time, he had to be home before the time deadline they had established. Excuses for being late were not accepted. Praise would be offered for accomplishments but punishment would also occur for failure to meet expectations. Praise would not be given for simple compliance with regulations. Parents and grandparent would also provide training when interest was shown. His grandfather was an expert carpenter and Bob became quite a skilled user of tools. After age ten, Bob worked a part-time summer job in one of his Dad's stores. By sixteen, he actually managed one store for the summer.

He enjoyed lots of outdoor activities. He joined the Boy Scouts and became an Eagle scout after two years. Religious education was obtained through participation in church activities but was not heavily stressed.

In school, Bob had considerable success, although he always felt the pressure of having to do well – of somehow being at the head of his class. He remembers well, being taken by a teacher to a high hill and asked to scale it. Despite his fear, he remembered his grandfather's advice, told himself he could do it, and was the only one in his class who succeeded. He excelled not only in academic matters but in sports as well. Even in grammar school he evidenced considerable skill as a pitcher. In his senior year of high school he was elected the president of his class. During college he was nominated for All-American honors as a football quarterback.

His grandfather's reputation, the family's financial status and Bob's scholastic record enabled him to attend a top Ivy-League School where he majored in history and political science. After graduation he attended the business school and earned an MBA. Afterwards, he had no difficulty becoming employed at a major banking institution. Starting with a one-year management-training program, he successfully handled several assignments before becoming the Vice President of Marketing for the bank.

Controlling-Taking Characteristics in Comfortable Situations

Of major concern to someone who emphasizes this orientation is concerned about **getting things accomplished quickly**. With their tendency for **high confidence in their capability**, CTs believe that given dedicated energy and imagination any problem can be solved; and usually, if within their area of knowledge and experience, through their personal involvement.

CTs usually want to **take advantage of opportunities** that arise and consequently, **time is of the utmost importance** to them.

CTs delight in being **busy and having variety** in their work life. They like having a **lot of things to do** and accomplish. CTs like challenges.

Although they will rely on experts whom they trust, CTs have a tendency **to trust their own intuitive assessment** of situations.

CTs get great satisfaction from being able to marshal the resources necessary to make things happen and they like **to be in charge**. This feeling is also accompanied by an enjoyment of the power of decision-making and the delight in functioning autonomously.

Controlling-Taking Characteristics in Conflict or Crisis Situations

When **conflict** occurs CTs are **willing to confront differences** in a **confident** and assertive manner in order to **convince others of the value of their position and** ultimately to get their way.

CTs enjoy arguing positions, with a tendency to **state their views and feelings openly and directly**. The give and take from a good argument helps them **appreciate the value of other viewpoints** and can assist them in making decisions.

In **stress** situations, CTs want to restore control immediately, to **take actions quickly** and to be **involved in a number of situations personally.** They value **prompt and competent handling of difficult situations.**

Controlling-Taking Assets

- Expressing desires directly to eliminate confusion
- Indicating specifically what one is looking for
- Making decisions quickly
- Letting others know where they stand with you
- Expressing confidence that other people can achieve what is asked of them (I can do that. I know it can be done)
- Being willing to take risks
- Staying on top of what is happening
- Acting directly to show what is needed
- Confronting differences
- Taking charge when there is no action
- Exercising initiative to get things done
- Acting independently
- Gathering resources and directing them against the task

Additional Considerations about the Controlling-Taking Style

Sometimes, if you offer ideas and suggestions to someone who favors this orientation, you are rebuffed or ignored. If you consider that the focus of the CT style involves concentrating on what the CT person wants to achieve – immediately if possible – this behavior becomes a more understandable. Thus, a CT person needs to feel that your input is related to his/her current interests. Indeed, CTs may view offers and suggestions as criticism, as implying they are unable to reach the proper conclusions or solutions on their own. Unless they specifically request input or experience problems beyond their capability or available time, CT's are likely to reject offers of assistance or respond to such offers with irritation.

It is not that CTs don't value the help, but simply, that it is not asked for – CTs believe they can handle it by themselves. It never occurs to them to ask for help. Of course, the person offering it, hoping to be perceived as contributing, may feel unappreciated. Nevertheless, the best course for the giver would be to ask if help is needed or wanted – and to accept the answer.

Thus, an important key for understanding people who prefer this orientation is to recognize the sense of initiative and pride in their own capabilities. Often, after you have made a suggestion you are likely to hear "I already thought (or did) that" or "I've gone beyond that to . . . ."

If your help is requested, it is expected almost immediately, especially if you have the expertise that is required to achieve a resolution. After all, if you are the expert, you should know. When one of the authors offered alternatives to a CT style CEO, he remarked, "What do you recommend? If I am faced with options, I want the best answer! And that's what I'm paying you for!" There is little patience for a more cautious approach.

In another company, the Vice President for Manufacturing agreed to a test of the effectiveness of more detailed planning. Two lines were established, both to manufacture the same item. The " Big Plan" group was still planning six months later, but the "Little Plan" group had started manufacturing after three months. Nevertheless, by the end of the year both groups had reached equal progress, but the number of production errors in the Little Plan group was twice that of the Big Plan group. At the end of one and a half years, the Big Plan group's production rate exceeded that of the Little Plan group by a factor of almost two.

Despite these results, the VP would not agree to a change in the planning process – stating that he could not wait for six months before any production occurred.

This need for a fast tempo can often create irritation when

---

others impede it, as if they were blocking the possibility for action. In short, acting by itself is prized by CTs, and even if wrong, CTs can quickly reverse and try another path. Reluctance to move is often viewed as inability to get things done. But the speed of ideation can also be a boon for creativity, for not being satisfied when things are not working as anticipated can encourage innovation. Since with this style there is also a heavily pragmatic outlook, if something works elsewhere, the CT wants to know about it and see it implemented in his or her own organization. Thus, if involved in strategic planning, CTs view *the* future as more short ranged – almost tactical in nature.

In addition, one should appreciate something about the way such a person reacts to the environment. Changing conditions and situations are stimulating and there is a ready flow of ideas and reactions that are likely to be expressed. There is less attuning to one's internal world, flowing with the feeling and searching for the profundity of meaning. Thought runs and is apprehended intuitively in relation to the surrounding context. Therefore, the CT often deprecates failure in others to be so open and direct. This CT attitude can feel threatening to those who deal with experience in wholly different ways (especially SG & CH modes).

Nevertheless, the CT can respect a confident refusal to be rushed, providing an explanation is given that makes sense. For example, in one major retailing corporation, the President would ask and expect prompt and accurate answers to his requests. At one meeting, he turned to the Financial Vice President and asked, "What's the latest situation on inventories versus sales?" The VP countered, "Do you want an answer you can count on, or just a feeling?" "One I can count on!" the president replied. The VP stated, "I'll have it for you by Monday," to which the President added, "Okay – by 11:00 a.m." Both men were highly CT in their orientations but realized that to meet the other's demands the delay was necessary. Confidence and strength carried the day – both men respected one another but needed to assess the other's convictions and style.

CHAPTER 8

THE CONSERVING-HOLDING ORIENTATION (CH)

The LIFO® Styles	
SUPPORTING/GIVING	*Mainly about people* ADAPTING/DEALING
Self Referenced	*Other Referenced*
CONSERVING/ HOLDING	CONTROLLING/TAKING *Mainly about task*

Pekka Virtanen

A CONSERVING-HOLDING CASE STUDY

Pekka Virtanen is the Financial Director of a business that supports the development and manufacture of wireless technologies. His firm, located in the suburbs of Helsinki, has grown rapidly in the wake of the success of a major Finnish company in the telecommunications field. Prior to joining this company three years earlier, Pekka had worked in the accounting and audit department of a large energy firm. During twelve years there he had obtained a strong foundation in financial analysis and management. When the chance to join a fast growing company in an exciting new field arose, Pekka was initially very cautious. But after a careful examination of the pros and cons, he decided to make the change.

Pekka is exceptionally conscientious and thorough in whatever he undertakes. He likes to use a systematic and methodical manner to accomplish his tasks. His staff has learned that Pekka pays careful attention to details. Given that tendency, the senior management team relies on him to make certain that financial analyses are accurate and that business activities are being measured against agreed upon plans.

At times some of the managers in the company feel that Pekka is too control-oriented. He insists on careful planning and analysis of all action plans, and this sometimes does not coincide with the needs of others to act spontaneously based on their instincts about market conditions. This style of operating is especially difficult for the sales and marketing people as Pekka can be perceived as being more concerned about administrative matters than seeing things from the customer's viewpoint.

People who work for Pekka expect that he is clear about what he wants from them. They also believe that he tries to treat people fairly and objectively. However, sometimes they are concerned that he expects his staff to work to the same high standards that he sets for himself. Since Pekka keeps somewhat of a formal distance from his subordinates it is hard to get to know him personally. While not unfriendly, he is primarily interested in getting tasks completed so his attentions are focused on following the progress of work and getting to completion of assignments.

During meetings Pekka is seen as a serious and hardworking team member. However, he typically speaks only when he has something useful and relevant to say. His comments demonstrate his concerns for an organized and logical approach to dealing with issues. He will also question the quality of information that is available for assessment and decision-making.

When the company was recently examining the potential acquisition of a rival, Pekka's careful method of dealing with change became evident. He needed factual information and time to digest the data before feeling comfortable with his decision. Generally, when new approaches are being discussed Pekka can be expected to question them and may, in fact, appear somewhat critical while he is assessing the impact of the data. His management team have learned to understand that this approach may not necessarily indicate a negative position about a particular subject. Rather, it is the way Pekka needs to get his arms around the data before making up his own mind.

Sometimes Pekka's colleagues think he is too much of a perfectionist in his expectations of others. This was a trait that was prized during his days as an auditor at his former employer, although you can be sure that the subjects of his investigations perceived Pekka as fussy and nitpicking on details. However, this also means that sometimes his subordinates feel they can never please him. The sense of control and review that Pekka requires can create the impression that his team is never fully trusted, or that delegation is always incomplete.

When Pekka is put under stress or is threatened, he reacts in a deliberate and objective manner. He will first study the situation and determine priorities that need to be established. Then he will examine the risks and benefits of alternative approaches before determining his own position. Pekka will fall back on organizational processes, procedures and reporting guidelines to support the way forward in a crisis. Given his dedication and involvement in trying to reach solutions, you can also count on him to check with and value the expertise of others. What does suffer during difficult times, however, can be his seeming concern for employees' morale, as Pekka will be more focused on the task at hand than on the feelings of others.

———

Family Background

Pekka was born in the country's capital of Helsinki. As an only child of working parents he went to day care and then through the public school system. His father worked as an engineer and his mother as a schoolteacher. They lived in a small apartment in the center of Helsinki until he was ten years old and then they moved to a row house in the suburbs. During his formative years Pekka grew up with a great deal of independence, travelling by himself to school, sports clubs and friend's houses on the public transportation system. Upon completion of high school and an excellent performance on entrance exams he attended the leading university for economics and finance where he obtained his degree. He accepted a job with a large company in the energy field following graduation, but before starting and with the company's agreement, Pekka took a year off backpacking around Europe.

Today, Pekka is married to a dentist and they have one small child. He and his wife consider themselves as having a high standard of living. While both parents work hard they make it home each night for dinner as a family. They also cherish their seven weeks of annual vacation time together, looking forward to their winter ski trip in Europe and summer holidays at their lakeside cabin.

Pekka has witnessed the development of Finland into a major competitive force in several industries. He appreciates that the capital city has become a more open and cosmopolitan place especially since Finland joined the European Union several years ago. He and his wife believe they are very fortunate to work in stimulating fields and at the same time enjoy the fruits of their labors.

The Conserving-Holding Characteristics in Comfortable Situations

he Conserving-Holding person is most **interested in minimizing loss and optimizing gains.** At the same time this type of person has a keen interest in **getting things done accurately and thoroughly.**

CHs favor a **cautious approach** and use **analysis, planning, systems, and routines** to minimize risk and assure that everything is being handled properly. They therefore value care, organization, and good systematic habits highly.

CHs feel that it's a lot easier and often less expensive to **make sure** one knows what one wants to do, has surveyed alternatives to determine the best and most economical way to do a task, and has planned how to get the work done with the resources available. They like to **follow-up** systematically to assure that things have been done as planned.

CHs believe that things can get out of hand because people lose focus and concentration. They can become distracted, instead of **staying with one thing fully** until it is finished.

They are comfortable with and like to **follow policies and procedures rigorously.** Once systems have been established CHs favor following them until someone else proves there is a better way or one that makes more sense.

With CHs, a great deal of **attention is paid to facts and details.** Consequently, in their work they are concerned about having appropriate documentation and information retrieval systems.

CHs believe that to avoid difficulties it is important to **maintain formal and objective relations** with people and to try to avoid **being distracted by emotions.**

Conserving-Holding Characteristics in Conflict or Crisis Situations

In disagreements CHs pay keen **attention to the accuracy of facts and information, the quality of reasoning involved and the systematic covering of all aspects** of the issue. They prefer using a **calm and deliberate manner** in such situations and are reluctant to engage in emotional behavior. Typically CH's would rather spend time on research before becoming involved in arguments.

Once engaged in argumentation, **only better facts or superior logic will prevail** in overcoming CH views. The CH feels no rush to achieve resolution to conflict and can hang on doggedly despite pressure from others.

A similar deliberateness, emphasizing research and analysis, characterizes the CH approach to extreme **stress** situations. Once understanding of what is involved is clear, CHs make attempts to **organize a planned approach** in order to remedy the situation. Information is gathered as efforts progress to **assess what is involved**, to **keep track** of events, and to evaluate performance. CHs favor **long-term resolutions** to finding immediate relief.

Conserving-Holding Assets

- Double-checking what has happened
- Establishing a clear structure for work efforts
- Carefully analyzing what is involved before acting
- Documenting what happens
- Calling attention to the need for information before making decisions
- Expending effort to assure clarity of instructions
- Thoroughly reviewing all the details involved
- Providing consistent behavior
- Requesting appropriate planning and organization for meetings

- Adhering to schedules and budgets
- Attention to costs when considering proposals
- Maintaining calmness when crises arise
- Assuring objective and fair evaluations
- Making sure everything is treated in an organized and systematic fashion
- Checking the logic and facts that underlie a position
- Encouraging attention to details
- Assuring adherence to policies and procedures

Additional Considerations for the Conserving-Holding Style

If you might feel critical about CH behaviors (CTs and ADs are most likely to), it may pay to be reminded of the unique qualities reflected in this style. CH's have deep respect for knowledge, for the ability to appraise situations calmly, to know what information is needed in order to understand what is happening, and to weigh consequences carefully before reacting. While CH excesses may result in what appears to be procrastination and endless fondness for detail, consider what one gains from consistency, from being able to count on predictable and organized behavior. The CH's quality of thinking and its logical implications are highly useful. There is also great interest derived from the richness of detail when the CH fleshes out events and issues. Thus, one is not likely to get quick and casual treatment from a CH, but treatment that is deliberate and thoughtful.

This style loves structure and has an immense appreciation of rules, regulations, and procedures. This means that CHs believe their behavior can be justified by what is known and accepted and reflects whole-hearted commitment to that framework. They may have concern about deviations that do not make sense or appear to be someone's whims, especially if they violate the rules. While this may seem antithetical to creativity, CHs also contribute to new ideas through their interest in considering alternative pathways for determining that ideas meet agreed upon criteria. Discoveries in scientific research have been the consequence of such style usage. It also means that CHs value plans as well as close follow-up to assess the anticipated benefits. CHs don't like slip-ups to occur. Think of which style you would like to have at the other end of the rope if you were climbing a mountain. Omissions are less likely to occur, payments will be made on time, cost consciousness will be evidenced and questions raised about the proposed benefits as contrasted to the risks involved.

As a counterbalance to the impulsiveness of others, as a measure of whether actions make sense, and as a passionate seeker of information, CHs make a needed contribution in a team, providing team members frame work with a sense of time that leverages the values represented by the CH style. In collaboration CHs make contributions that elaborate on and complete the picture hastily sketched by others, helping to assure accountability.

For example, when the CH style combines with the Supporting-Giving style, idealistic intentions are more likely to be realized than by the Supporting-Giving style alone, since CHs will help ensure that deeds support desires – that one lives as one says. With the Controlling-Taking style, CHs can provide the kind of support that ensures focus in an extremely integrated and organized fashion, that enables frameworks to be established that are both opportunistic and practical, and that works toward the coordination and integration of disparate aspects for results. With Adapting-Dealing support, CH flexibility can be added to assure that structures relate to changing conditions and are not designed in the abstract but relate to the concerns and needs of others – as well as providing more consistency for the AD style to reinforce the identity of personal convictions.

CHAPTER 9

THE ADAPTING-DEALING ORIENTATION (AD)

```
┌─────────────────────────────────────────────────┐
│              ┌─────────────────────┐             │
│              │   The LIFO® Styles  │             │
│              └─────────────────────┘             │
│   ┌──────────────────────┬──────────────────────┐│
│   │        Mainly  ↑     │                      ││
│   │        about         │                      ││
│   │        people        │  ADAPTING/           ││
│   │   SUPPORTING/GIVING   │  DEALING             ││
│   │                      │                      ││
│   │ Self Referenced      │      Other Referenced││
│   │ ←────────────────────┼────────────────────→ ││
│   │                      │                      ││
│   │  CONSERVING/HOLDING   │  CONTROLLING/TAKING  ││
│   │                      │                      ││
│   │        Mainly        │                      ││
│   │        about   ↓     │                      ││
│   │        task          │                      ││
│   └──────────────────────┴──────────────────────┘│
└─────────────────────────────────────────────────┘
```

Roberta Amara

AN ADAPTING-DEALING CASE STUDY

Roberta Amara is the Director of Human Resources for a large international oil company. She is affable, seems to know everyone, and generally exhibits a cheerful outlook and an enthusiastic attitude when anyone contacts her.

Roberta has been in several of the major divisions of the company, beginning as a personnel assistant, serving on recruiting and compensation staffs, assuming a personnel directorship in one of the divisions, and last January was appointed the Corporate Director of Human Resources.

She has a reputation for dealing with people and difficult situations smoothly, with finesse. An excellent third party consultant in conflicts, she uses tact and diplomacy to minimize tensions and achieve working compromises. Despite considerable resistance to her promotion (some managers felt she was too young for the job), she has been able to win opponents to her side. Possessing a ready wit and a pleasant sense of humor, she feels at home in all kinds of groups, able to deal effectively with union representatives, operations managers, or top management.

Roberta doesn't sit in her office but circulates widely around the company, talking to people wherever she goes. People find her a good listener and enjoy sharing experiences with her. As a result, she has not only made a lot of friends but has amassed a good deal of intelligence about many corporate areas.

Because there is an exceptionally high degree of cohesiveness and morale in their department, Roberta's staff members say they feel like members of a family. In addition, they have opportunities to be in the forefront of many new experiments. She has a reputation for being courteous and appreciative in her treatment of staff members at all levels. Roberta is able to see the "best" in people. She is liberal in the use of positive remarks, even when criticizing behavior.

Roberta seems able to sell others on support for special projects in Human Resources. She enjoys an enviable budget for its services. She insists that staff members keep in touch with their respective "constituents and clients." It is important for them to keep her informed about the groundswell of attitudes and opinions. She likes to have "trial balloons" of new ideas and opportunities to test them before committing to a full-scale project.

Human resources staff personnel are expected to sound out new ideas with key people before making formal proposals.

Sometimes, she is viewed by others as overly solicitous and

too concerned about others' opinions. It appears as if she is too ready to back off from confrontations and to modify her views if she receives any negative comments or reactions. While Roberta can handle a conflict deftly, she does not press her point strongly enough in a climate of threatening or critical views. Some managers feel that she has retreated from strong positions unnecessarily. At times, the person with the last opinion can affect Roberta's decision disproportionately.

Under pressure, Roberta is usually tense, concerned about her reputation and possible disapproval. She doesn't relax until everything is under control and she has the assurance of positive regard from those who are important to her. Yet, when serious crises occur she exhibits a flexible and encouraging approach, a willingness to entertain novel ideas and to experiment with new approaches. Generally optimistic about the ultimate outcome, she can sometimes promise more than she can deliver.

Her career in personnel almost ended with her assignment to the compensation area. Her boss expected her to devote her energy to research and administration of paperwork, including an annual survey of competitor salaries. After a few months Roberta seemed somewhat depressed. Reports were delayed, incurring complaints from the boss. At that point she requested a transfer to the recruiting area, her previous department.

When questioned by her boss, Roberta told him that she found contact with prospective employees, managers and colleagues highly stimulating and satisfying. She did not enjoy work with numbers and reports. "I don't feel I was born for that," she said. "If you think I am causing you too much trouble, I could go back to recruiting or even leave the company." The boss wisely agreed to a compromise, assigning an assistant to handle the financial details and using Roberta to deal with managers concerning wage policies and salary reviews.

Two months later, Roberta felt like a new person. Her usual manner was evident – once again she approached work with zeal and interest. As a buffer to the Compensation Director, who tended to be more of a technical expert, she provided liaison skills, which did much to enhance the effectiveness of the department.

Roberta is equally outgoing in her social life. She has many friends and acquaintances and is active in several groups. An amateur actress, she belongs to a volunteer theatre group that performs several plays a year. She was recently appointed to the Mayor's Committee on Employment for the Disadvantaged and recruited several prominent people as additional members.

Family Background

Roberta's family was a well-established and prominent one in the capital city of their country of origin. Considerable land-holdings generated sufficient wealth to send her father to a University in the United States, where he majored in petroleum engineering. While there, he met Roberta's mother, a music major from the same country. Married abroad, the parents returned to their native country, where the father joined a large multinational oil company. Through the years, her father rose to become managing director of the local company and became a senior vice-president. Roberta's mother continued her musical career, establishing a reputation as a fine concert pianist. Roberta and her three sisters rarely lacked for anything. The family was constantly concerned about the image they projected and from her earliest days she was constantly reminded that she had to set an example for others – "if you don't do that, other people won't think well of you!" was a frequent formula for controlling her behavior. She felt it was very difficult to be an independent person since her family was so well known in the community. At the same time, she felt pressure to do well and become someone who is important.

Numerous parties and social events were part of family life. Both parents ensured that their children were present and shared in the experience. Despite such pressures, there was a generally friendly climate where everyone was expected to join in and participate. The extended family of relatives also assumed major importance in the children's lives. Brilliant conversation, humorous remarks, and laughter are remembered vividly as a constant part of her childhood.

Roberta attended private school and was provided with music and dancing lessons, schooled in English, French and Spanish. Popular in school, she was the center of many groups, the star singer in several musical productions, and a member of the swimming team. When she was sent to her father's university, she enjoyed feeling free of the constant wariness generated by her family's reputation, and she became more spontaneous. Her Latin-American background and her personality gained her access to many groups. She joined a sorority and was elected president in her senior year. In addition, Roberta was a member of the women's swimming team. Her college years were full of fun. Academic progress followed and she became torn between a career in music and one in psychology.

Following her graduation, Roberta's father secured a position for her in the personnel department of the oil company and she progressed rapidly. When an opening developed at the corporate headquarters in the United States, she leapt at the opportunity and has been living there ever since.

The Adapting-Dealing Style Characteristics in Comfortable Situations

The basic consideration of the Adapting-Dealing person is the desire to **be liked and admired by others**. Thus, ADs have a keen **interest in being included** by others in activities and groups.

ADs **enjoy working with people** and find the challenge of new relationships exciting. An AD knows intuitively that once one gets to understand people one can influence them. Therefore, ADs make efforts to observe others as well as to be friendly and sociable. ADs realize that understanding how a person thinks and feels, what he/she values and is sensitive to provides impor-

—

tant keys to gaining his or her acceptance and collaboration. They readily express their **empathic understanding** of others.

ADs have also learned that it is important to **keep oneself open to new experiences,** to be **enthusiastic** and willing to **experiment,** and to be **flexible.** When one approach fails ADs have the feeling that there are others that can work. Even in failure situations, the AD believes that if he or she keeps an eye open, cues will be discovered that will help lead to developing more successful ways of getting things done.

ADs put emphasis on presenting their points and ideas with **tact** and care. Life is viewed as a matter of give and take, so ADs **enjoy negotiating** and dealing with people. Generally they believe that it pays to go through life **making as many friends as possible** and keeping **one's options** open.

ADs value a friendly and **optimistic** attitude as a basic asset to achieve success. They try whenever possible to communicate positive feelings about others, to be generous in **offering compliments,** and to make statements of acknowledgment and **appreciation** for efforts that others have made.

Highly **sensitive to feelings and social amenities,** for ADs **humor** and light touches are appreciated and they utilize them whenever possible.

Adapting-Dealing Characteristics in Conflict or Crisis Situations

A **win-win** attitude is reflected in how ADs deal with conflicts and disagreements. They readily demonstrate a willingness to compromise and achieve mutually satisfactory agreements. ADs are **attentive to the other person's viewpoint,** acknowledge its value and try to utilize understanding to present convincing arguments for their own position. **Critical and demeaning comments are rarely employed.** ADs make a major effort be persuasive without antagonizing the other person. **Humor and other tension-relieving remarks** are used to defuse tension and preserve relationships. In **stress** situations ADs are very attentive to morale as well as resolving difficulties.

ADs are **flexible and open to new ideas.** They are willing to experiment with any approach that could be successful. Finally, they tend to maintain an **optimistic outlook** and communicate to others, both staff and superiors.

Adapting-Dealing Assets

- Expressing appreciation for efforts
- Sensing feelings and acknowledging them
- Expressing empathy
- Listening to new ideas in a positive way
- Encouraging flexibility and experimentation
- Building harmony and friendly relationships
- Providing information on how people are likely to feel if treated in a particular way
- Awareness of customer needs and attitudes
- Willingness to see the other side of the issue
- Negotiating in a positive and win-win manner
- Expressing remarks that make people feel good about themselves
- Providing a sense of fun in what is being done
- Expressing and encouraging enthusiasm and optimism
- Willing to approach changes in a positive manner
- Dealing positively with the public and other groups
- Willing to try something first before accepting or rejecting it
- Tactful and diplomatic in dealing with delicate situations

Additional Considerations of the Adapting-Dealing Style

Some people do not appreciate the AD orientation. Unfortunately, the term "wheeler-dealer" sometimes seems to stick in people's minds for this style. It can be argued that a better generic title for this style may have been chosen; however, let's set the story to right.

As a means of broadening your view of the AD style, imagine what life would be like without the ameliorative and pleasant effects of tactful and sensitive remarks that characterize this orientation. In such a world, phone calls would be like the type one author occasionally experienced at home when his son's friend would telephone. The caller, seeking the author's sixteen-year-old son would often say "Larry." When the author askrf, "Who is this?" the answer would follow: "I'd like to talk with Larry." There's no "hello," no identification, no "Thanks." The son's friends entered and left rooms without any acknowledgment of who is there – no greeting and no goodbye. People didn't seem to exist save for the immediacy of the teenagers' needs or tasks.

Think too, of the reactions to your own work or contributions. Without the AD style, there would be no complimentary words, appreciation, recognition, or spontaneous remarks that would show you that your good points or accomplishments have been noticed. People would also say whatever they wanted to without regard for your attitudes, feelings and sensitivities. After all, from their point of view, what difference does it make? The point was made, wasn't it?

In presenting a new idea or selling a product people wouldn't hesitate to deprecate old ideas, criticize products you have purchased or ridicule your espoused attitudes and beliefs. They would concentrate only on their ideas and what they want to say. If you didn't understand, they would simply repeat what they said before rather than trying a different approach or (heaven forbid) asking what would help you to understand. When new ideas are introduced, these people would criticize them immediately, finding whatever flaws existed rather than playing with the possibilities, exploring the implications and imagining what would happen if the ideas could be realized – in short, forget about creative thinking.

If disagreements occurred, people wouldn't bother to listen to you, try to find out what you're concerned about and the reasons supporting your position, or try to acknowledge what you've been saying. They would simply look for the first opportunity to press their point home.

People who have no investment in the AD orientation would seldom bother to demonstrate any interest in what is happening to you, failing to recall anything about your personal life, family or experiences. They wouldn't share much in the experiences you're having together, enjoy humor, laugh at jokes, or examine other views that might lend perspective to what is being experienced. When visiting other countries they would behave exactly as they behaved at home, not interested in learning the language, appreciating the customs, taking account of special sensitivities or telling people what they enjoyed about their stay with them and their country.

It sounds kind of stark, doesn't it? It is the adapting-dealing behavior and attitudes that give a totally different character to relationships and provide a tenor to experience that makes it enjoyable and reduces tension and antagonisms. In fact, many of the different training experiences that are offered in the business world emphasize the necessity to acquire adapting-dealing skills. Sensitivity training, active listening, feedback training, managing interpersonal relationships, synectics, creative problem-solving (looking for new alternatives and experimenting with ideas), negotiation, managing conflict, communication workshops, selling and presentation skills are only some of the programs that are used to compensate for people's inabilities to employ these skills in their everyday lives. Deprecation and ridicule of this dimension seems totally unwarranted considering the added value provided by its presence in those who make effective use of it in their, work, home, and social situations. We feel strongly that we have to assure proper appreciation for this orientation, as well as for all of the others.

Perhaps some of the negative attitude concerning adapting-dealing comes from the judgment that it represents a rather shallow approach. We suspect this stems from observing an excessively defensive bit of behavior when the style is used to avoid conflict and emotional tension. This style has important deeper aspects that shouldn't be ignored. The depth of adapting-dealing attitudes is reflected in such feelings as, "Being different is okay," and "One ought to see what is of value in what other folks are saying," as well as the desire to find ways of integrating differences rather than proving to others that you are right. Clearly, these kinds of attitudes are useful for teamwork and collaboration. We may tend to overvalue orientations that are more power oriented, reflecting a status elevation of an adult's outlook as contrasted to a child's. Yet, the learnings of therapy seem to indicate that it is the proper integration of our child and adult selves that really leads to full utilization of our powers.

In world politics today, new approaches are required that place less emphasis on who is right or wrong, that appreciate strengths and assets of all sides, and that view things in terms of pluralities rather than either/or. The alternative to a cold war mentality (my idea versus yours) is the genuine recognition of another viewpoint, not one based on controlling the other person or country. The AD viewpoint would be one that focuses on integrating differences, sometimes without losing the other person's identity (creating a metaphorical salad) and sometimes integrating them into a new configuration (a metaphorical stew).

EFFECTIVE ORGANIZATIONS NEED ALL OF THE STYLES

An effective organization requires a balance of individuals who exhibit a variety of styles that, when combined, add value and move the business forward successfully. The following chart highlights the assets (productive use of strengths) and liabilities (when an individual uses his or her strengths to excess) of the four orientations. Looking at both sides of this behavioral "balance sheet" should reinforce the notion that a blend of styles within an organization is highly desirable.

STYLE	ASSETS	LIABILITIES (WHEN IN EXCESS)
Supporting-	Helpfulness	Gives too much help
Giving	Idealistic goals	Not practical
	Trusting	Gullible
	High standards	Overly critical
	Developmentally oriented	May sacrifice action for training
	Accepts direction	May not initiate enough
	Highly responsive	Over commits – can't say no
Controlling-	High initiating	Starts too many projects
Taking	Acts quickly	Impulsive
	Takes risks	Gambles with high stakes
	Confident	Arrogant
	Provides direction	Overly controlling
	Energizes others	Frenetic
	Accomplishment focused	May lose sight of values
	Assertive	Dominates conversation

STYLE	ASSETS	LIABILITIES (WHEN IN EXCESS)
Conserving-	Thorough	Involved in too much
Holding	Attention to detail	May become nitpicking
	Systematic	Too bound to procedure
	Analytical emphasis	Overly analytical – no action
	Composed	Unfeeling
	Tenacious	Can't let go – inflexible
	Highly organized	Compulsive
	Cost sensitive	Penurious
Adapting-	Flexible	Aimless
Dealing	Open to new ideas	Indiscriminate judgment
	Enthusiastic	Overly pushes for ideas
	Sensitive to feelings	Overly solicitous
	Communicates empathetically	Can't differ strongly
	Negotiates	May give away too much
	Has sense of humor	May minimize seriousness

STRENGTH APPRECIATION

The emphasis that The LIFO® Method places on strength appreciation reflects an AD orientation in the overall approach. There is no question that viewing differences from this kind of perspective powerfully alters attitudes in a constructive way during team building, especially after some kind of strength bombardment activity (or confirmation of strengths by others) and consideration of how individual strengths can be leveraged in team functioning.

In a similar way, for those of us who are practitioners and consultants, we hope we are providing full appreciation of all of the orientations in our seminars and organization development experiences – that we are not permitting the biases of our own major orientations to communicate that any particular orientation or style is to be preferred over any other. The major issue is how to make sure we are getting the most out of all of our orientations in business and personal life.

Summarizing The LIFO® Orientations and Styles

Now that you have a better understanding of the four LIFO® orientations, here is a summary chart that highlights how each orientation relates more generally to key aspects of your work life and perhaps also your non-work life.

	SUPPORTING-GIVING	CONTROLLING-TAKING	CONSERVING-HOLDING	ADAPTING-DEALING
Primary Need	Support/Con-tribute to collective goals	Set and achieve one's goals	Minimize risk of mistakes or damage to oneself	Adapt to the environment
Main Thrust	Improving	Directing	Co-ordinating	Brokering
Values	Quality	Achievement	Stability	Harmony
Approach to Organizational Processes	Improve and develop	Create	Maintain	Adapt
Use of Information	Shares	Creates	Stores	Collects
Focus and Mode of Communication	Sharing and group discussion	Verbal direction and Instruction to individuals and	Formal channels and in writing	Networking and individual conversation
People are valued for	Teamwork; Accepting collective responsibility	Results; Self motivation	Experience; Reliability and organization	Warmth; Sensitivity to other people
Time Perspective	Future	Present	Past	Other people's
Tend to undervalue	Independent action	Contribution of others	Need for innovation and change	Task requirements and constraints
Major Potential weakness	Letting things go	Impulsive	Stubborn	Appeasing

CHAPTER 10

CHECKING YOUR UNDERSTANDING OF LIFO® STYLES

In the next chapter you will have a chance to complete a questionnaire that gives you feedback on your own style mix. At this point you should have a pretty good feeling for the four LIFO® styles. You may want to check your understanding, so the feedback you get about yourself will be better understood.

Next to each number, indicate the style most likely to make that statement (SG, CT, CH or AD) by putting a checkmark in the appropriate column. In some cases, there may be two style categories that would seem appropriate. Think of the reasons that justify your answers and check back in the earlier chapter if you have any doubts.

	SG	CT	CH	AD
1. I like to feel in charge of things – to take command and get things done.				
2. Cohesiveness among my employees is what I value most.				
3. I take pride in developing people and seeing them go on to bigger and better jobs.				
4. If I offend someone, I'm very concerned.				
5. I speak directly about my thoughts and feelings.				

6. I can take a strong stand, but when I'm up against stiff opposition I can shift my position to achieve good will.				
7. When people disagree with me, I usually give in rather than have an argument.				
8. I can take criticism readily and make use of it.				
9. I have compassion for people and am willing to show it.				
10. The customer I have most difficulty with is the indecisive one.				
11. I know what to say to people to motivate them to work well.				
12. Most people feel I am a pretty cooperative person.				
13. It is fun and easy for me to meet new people.				
14. I tend to panic under pressure.				
15. I believe in letting a person know where he/she stands.				
16. I think most people can be trusted fully.				
17. I am likely to check with other people for their advice before acting.				
18. I have a difficult time trying to read between the lines of what people say.				
19. When there are strong disagreements, I try to see how we can both get something from the situation.				
20. I feel you have to watch employees closely or they will try to get away with something.				

Now, compare your answers with the following answer list:

1. CT	8. CH	15.CT
2. AD	9. SG with AD	16. SG
3. SG	10. CT	17. SG and AD
4. AD	11. AD with CT	18. CH
5. CT	12. SG	19. AD
6. CT with AD	13. AD	20. CT with CH
7. SG	14. SG	

These statements are only samples but if you can do well with them, keep practicing in all kinds of circumstances such as conversations, TV shows, books, and the like. With practice you will soon become expert in making appropriate identifications of other people's styles.

Style Confusion

Sometimes confusions occur between orientation styles because the names seem similar. One of the pairs most misunderstood is the difference between SG and AD styles.

At first glance it is easy to be confused. If one only pays attention to the labels of Supporting-Giving and Adapting-Dealing it seems like both styles are concerned with people. In some ways, yes, but in other ways, they represent vastly different ways of relating to people.

The **SG** concern is more remote. In terms of ideals and values, the person emphasising this orientation believes in doing things he or she believes will be of benefit to others, to foster better relationships in a community, to advance commitment to beliefs, to provide assistance when asked or judged as needed. The motivation for an SG's action stems from a desire to be a good person, to operate within the spirit of the major tenets and values one holds dear.

Thus, an SG does something almost as a commandment – in

the biblical sense – and does this from the SG's own sense of values. An SG offers sympathy to others when needed, but may not communicate empathically. He can be willing to prevent another from abortion because the other person will be violating what he believes is vital, not with any consideration for the life space and feelings of the person seeking abortion. The SG believes everyone ought to participate equally in teams, even if the other person believes he/she functions best independently. The SG's focus in a relationship is mainly from her own frame of reference and therefore, events and acts are judged from this perspective.

The **AD** is primarily concerned with relationship – with striving to be in tune with others – not to impose one's values on them but to enter into the experiential world of the other, to understand and feel how events and experiences are being sensed by the other – and to communicate with full awareness of that internal world. Empathy – the sharing of awareness with another, the acknowledgment of what it must mean to have that experience and to somehow work with that – that is the essence of the AD approach.

The SG operating from a defined value system tends to be less flexible than the AD. It is important for the person who emphasizes this orientation to somehow influence others to become part of his or her value system. The AD can see merits in alternative approaches, believes in providing options – as long as it doesn't disrupt relationships – and believes in accepting differences and actively trying to work with them. The SG may also have this as one of his or her important values, but is less likely to behave sensitively in this way. To do that takes the full understanding of how people feel and understand, and this requires the willingness to risk understanding others in their own terms.

To be sure, the combination of SG and AD styles can be very powerful and be evidenced in a friendly, co-operative, playful, respectful, sensitive and easy-going manner. Yet, there would be times when some internalized conflicts could arise. When, for example, would principle allow complete flexibility? And when one desires to gain acceptance, will that mean giving up what one really believes?

The impacts of the two styles are likely to be different. SGs may tend more to be serious, pleasant and respectful but less playful. ADs may seem to take things too lightly and not stand up for what they really believe in.

Instruction from an SG point of view is emphatic – one is trying to teach someone what is important and what he or she absolutely needs to know. From an AD point of view, one begins with rapport, to understand what the other person knows and to provide experiences to enable him/her to understand it so it "speaks to" that person. The concern for checking understanding by sensing how the learner is receiving instruction is more AD. Testing for understanding through examinations is more of an SG mode. Responding to requests for help is more SG. For the AD, it may be dependent on the relationship – you help your friends or those who can benefit you most first

SGs follow willingly those who inspire, who seem to live up to their ideals and values. ADs follow more those who are friendly, approving, and influential.

Certainly aspects of both styles are valuable in relationships and as might be expected, can be useful when incorporated into other styles as well, albeit with different intensities and combinations. We will examine such combinations in a later chapter.

The Power of Reading Clues about Another Person's LIFO® Styles

You should now have a good understanding about the LIFO® styles. How can you use that knowledge to start improving your relationships with people on a daily basis? Your colleagues at work, your boss, and your life partner have always been providing clues about their styles. For some of them you have sensed a pattern of behavior, but you have not had a framework to understand how it all fits together and to anticipate how **they** would like to be treated. Remember the golden rule of the LIFO® Method?

With your knowledge of LIFO® styles you can now read clues, i.e. patterns of behavior, make a judgment of what LIFO® styles are being exhibited, and then use your strengths to accomplish your goal. The following table, "How to Relate to Other People according to their LIFO® Orientation," will give you some very specific hints on how this can be done.

HOW TO RELATE TO PEOPLE ACCORDING TO THEIR STYLE

	SG	CT	CH	AD
How to communicate with a person according to each style	• Stress worth-while causes • Appeal to their ideals • Ask for their help • Show concern • Emphasize self-development	• Offer opportunity to achieve results • Give more responsibility • Challenge • Provide resources to allow for achievement • Give authority	• Present ideas as low risk • Give opportunity to be analytical • Exercise logic • Use familiarity, routine, and structure • Tie new things to old	• Offer a chance to do things with others • Use humorous appeals • Let them know you are pleased • Provide opportunities to be in the spotlight
Most effective environment for each style	• Respecting • Mutually supporting • Reassuring • Committed to people	• Competitive • Clear, unambiguous • Risk-taking • Opportunistic	• Unemotional • Predictable • Structured • Practical	• Social • Changing • Growing • Optimistic
Least effective environment for each style	• Betrayal • Personal criticism • Ridicule • Failure • Lack of support	• No resources • Authority countermanded • Responsibility diminished • No challenges • Can't control factors which affect results	• Constantly changing rules and policies • Highly emotional • Premature decision-making • Failure to be taken seriously	• Critical authority • Unfriendly co-workers • Routines and details • Firm schedules and supervision
How to be the most effective Boss to someone of each style	• Give recognition, trust and appreciation • Mutual goal-setting • Be accessible • Try to share • Be dependable • Be fair	• Be confident • Provide autonomy • Reward results • Indicate firm boundaries, but appreciate initiative • Listen, but be decisive • Argue on equal basis	• Have a methodical approach • Provide detail when briefing • React objectively • Provide reasons for decisions • Be consistent	• Be friendly • Be informative as to own feelings • Encourage other's efforts • Be flexible • Display sense of humor
How to help and influence effectively a Boss of each style	• Demonstrate worth • Show loyalty • Be sincere • Be team-oriented	• Respond quickly to his/her direction • Establish clear objectives • Show personal initiative • Deal directly with challenges and questions	• Be respectful of the hierarchy • Conform to procedures • Be logical in presenting ideas • Pay attention to detail	• Be sociable • Try new ideas • Be tactful and diplomatic • Cultivate mutually helpful connections

CHAPTER 11

WHAT IS YOUR LIFO® PROFILE?

In order to interact more effectively with others you must start with a clear understanding about your own strengths. Change in your behavior is not possible unless you know and accept your starting position.

- What are your preferred behaviors?
- Why do you act in certain ways?

If you were to take a LIFO® Seminar under the guidance of a trained LIFO® professional, the first thing you would do is complete the LIFO® Survey. Your answers to this questionnaire provide the basis for feedback that enables you to interpret your behavioral patterns. In this book we provide you with a modified version of the LIFO® Survey. It has been designed to give you a good sense of your major LIFO® styles. It does not offer some of the depth and richness you would get from a LIFO® workshop, but as a starting point it will give you important and useful feedback about yourself.

INSTRUCTIONS FOR COMPLETING THE LIFO® CHECKLIST

In the chart that follows you will find a LIFO® Checklist. You will notice that the list is divided into four columns, A through D, and into two parts. In the top half you will see a number of statements. In the bottom half you will see a list of adjectives. Read through the statements and adjectives. As you work through the list put a check in the box next to the statements and adjectives that best describe you. You can put check marks in as many boxes as you feel are appropriate. To get the most out of this exercise we suggest you apply the following guidelines:

1. Be honest with yourself.
2. Work through the statements and adjectives without thinking about them too much. Base your replies on your initial reactions.
3. Your reactions to the statements and adjectives are very much dependent on the situations against which they are applied. Therefore, if you want to understand your strengths as you use them at work, think about your office situation as you respond. Taking a different approach, you may want to respond to the statements and adjectives while thinking about your family setting or where you interact as part of a specific group e.g. a sports team, orchestra, etc.

When you have finished, add the number of boxes checked in the statements section and then in the adjectives section, putting the totals in the spaces provided. Then add the totals for the two sections across columns A through D in the spaces provided at the bottom of the page.

Now look at the two shaded rows where you added the number of boxes checked. Add the total number of boxes checked in columns A—D and enter the number below.

———

A

Check the Statements that best describe YOU

❑ I have to feel I am working on the most relevant project.

❑ I like to be an achiever, doing something to benefit people.

❑ I am willing to trust others' statements at face value.

❑ I allow others to feel important in determining the direction of what's happening.

❑ I make allowances for people and defend their rights.

No. boxes checked

Check the Adjectives that best describe YOU

❑ Thoughtful

❑ Idealistic

❑ Modest

❑ Trusting

❑ Cooperative

❑ Helpful

❑ Receptive

❑ Responsive

❑ Valued Contributor

❑ Loyal

No. boxes checked

B

Check the Statements that best describe YOU

❑ I like to be in control of relationships and steer the course of what's happening.

❑ I am quick to act and express a sense of urgency for others to act now.

❑ I enjoy the challenge of difficult situations and people.

❑ I am quick to move in and seize an opportunity or create one.

❑ I probe and press to get at hidden resistance.

No. boxes checked

Check the Adjectives that best describe YOU

❑   Directing

❑   Quick to Act

❑   Confident

❑   Seek Change

❑   Persuasive

❑   Forceful

❑   Competitive

❑   Risk-taking

❑   Persistent

❑   Urgent

No. boxes checked

C

Check the Statements that best describe YOU

❏ I rely heavily on data, analysis, and logic to make decisions.

❏ I outline the trade-offs of my position and the options for others.

❏ I thoroughly examine and study people's needs and situations.

❏ I work methodically, and consistently follow procedures and policies.

❏ I like working with the tried and true and getting the most out of what already exists.

No. boxes checked

Check the Adjectives that best describe YOU

❏ Tenacious

❏ Practical

❏ Economical

❏ Reserved

❏ Factual

❏ Steadfast

❏ Thorough

❏ Methodical

❏ Detail-oriented

❏ Analytical

No. boxes checked

D

Check the Statements that best describe YOU

❑ I use the light touch and personal charm to win people over.

❑ I am sensitive to and aware of others' feelings and what will please them.

❑ I am flexible in finding ways to satisfy other people.

❑ I am able to transact easily and fit in with all kinds of people.

❑ I am quick to change and adapt to new ideas and ways.

No. boxes checked

Check the Adjectives that best describe YOU

❑ Flexible

❑ Tactful

❑ Socially Skilful

❑ Youthful

❑ Enthusiastic

❑ Adaptable

❑ Inspiring

❑ Experimental

❑ Negotiating

❑ Animated

No. boxes checked

Now look at the two shaded rows where you added
the number of boxes checked.
Add the total number of boxes checked in
columns A - D and enter the number below.

A
Total number of boxes checked
B
Total number of boxes checked
C
Total number of boxes checked
D
Total number of boxes checked

Explaining Your Survey Scores

In the above checklist each of the four columns has statements or adjectives that refer to a corresponding LIFO® style.
They are as follows:

COLUMN	CORRESPONDING LIFO® STYLE
A	Supporting-Giving
B	Controlling-Taking
C	Conserving-Holding
D	Adapting-Dealing

The four orientations combine in each of us to form our Style
Mix. To examine your style mix, based on the questionnaire you
just completed, let us first consider the total number of boxes
you checked in each column, i.e. the figure at the bottom of the
page.

Your Most Preferred Style

If you find one of the four scores is much greater than any other, particular by a margin of four or five points or more, you probably use this style more than any other. This is what we call your Preferred Style. This is the orientation you rely on most and which produces most examples of your behavior. The statements and insights presented earlier in the book about that style are characteristic of your behavior.

Your Backup Style

The score that is next closest to your highest score represents a style that you might often use instead of the preferred style. It serves as an alternative style and also can modify how the preferred style is expressed in practice. It is called the Backup Style. In addition to having an effect on the most preferred style, you will be most likely to use it if you cannot have success with your preferred style.

For example, if you had a preferred Conserving-Holding orientation, influenced by a backup Controlling-Taking orientation, you will be less risk averse and have a keener sense of the opportunity cost of time than someone else whose Conserving strengths are more dominant. Or if, for example you have a preferred Controlling-Taking orientation influenced by a backup Adapting-Dealing orientation, you will be more inclined to test the acceptability of your ideas and actions and to acquire allies than someone in whom the Controlling strengths are more dominant.

Two things will determine the degree to which the influence of the backup is felt in the most preferred orientation:

- The relative importance you place on personal goals associated with the styles; and
- The situations in which you are conditioned to pursue a different personal goal from the ones you generally pursue.

———

For example, although you may have Controlling-Taking as your preferred orientation and you generally follow behaviors associated with that style, with your superiors you may behave in line with a backup Adapting-Dealing orientation since you want them to hold you in high personal esteem, as well as see you as active and competent.

Your Least Preferred Style

The column with the lowest score or least number of boxes checked is a style that would be the least characteristic of your attitudes and behaviors. Not surprisingly, this is called your Least Preferred Style. You would only be likely to use this style if the other ones were not helpful or if this was the only style appropriate for a specific situation. Others would not associate this style as characteristic of your typical behavior. The reason for its infrequent use may be that you have learned that using this behavior does not satisfy your psychological needs, or it may be that you have never tried to satisfy your needs using such behavior.

Blends

Sometimes your two highest scores are equal or separated by only a point or two. This means that your two main orientations are probably being used at the same intensity. They may even represent a merging of the two characteristics – what we call a Blend.

It is also possible to have a blend of three orientations with a single least preferred style. In this case the primary mode of behavior will reflect the influence of all three styles and may be also influenced by situations and roles.

You may be interested to note that typically for people who have taken the complete LIFO® survey about half use two styles regularly, a third use three styles and about 5% employ four styles equally. That leaves only about 10% with just one style. We therefore are not one style or another; rather, we tend to be one style and another.

Uniform Profiles

Lastly, it is possible that your scores may represent a uniform profile; that is, all four scores are within a point of two of each other (the 5% referred to above). You would not have any most preferred, backup or least preferred style. You seem to adapt to the requirements of many situations.

Deepening Your Interpretation through a LIFO® Seminar

Using the checklist you will have been able to obtain a general description of your LIFO® orientations. It is not a precise measurement, but a fair indication of your typical styles. If you were to attend a LIFO® seminar, however, this understanding would be significantly deepened in several ways.

Firstly, you would take a full LIFO® Survey as referred to earlier. This detailed survey has 18 descriptive statements, each with four endings. You are then asked to rank all of the endings in accordance with how you feel each applies to you. This ranking approach provides a great deal more information about your behavioral styles and how they relate to each other.

Secondly, given the full survey methodology you would receive important feedback about the congruency between how you intend (intention) to behave, how you actually behave (behavior) and what type of impact your behavior has on others. This valuable insight into *behavioral congruency* is a unique feature to the LIFO® method and is discussed further in the next chapter.

Thirdly, given a fuller understanding of your strengths profile you would be able to experience additional exercises in a LIFO® Workbook, as well as participate in discussions with other individuals to further your understanding of the concepts and how they apply to you.

Fourthly, the full LIFO® Survey can better take into account the fact that some people behave differently in different situations. As such, you would receive additional feedback as to how you tend to behave in both favorable and unfavorable (or adverse) conditions. It can be quite enlightening to see how our patterns can shift. You may recall that we describe these two situations earlier as follows:

Favorable Conditions are those where you feel comfortable, have relevant experience, needed resources and feel supported.

Unfavorable or Adverse Conditions are those situations where you may believe you are under psychological threat, or when you feel that things just are not going well for you. Unfavorable conditions may occur because you sense a threat to your ability to achieve your goals in the workplace (stress); or you cannot perform as you wish due to some pressure or threats from some person, group or people (conflict). The strengths of what in essence is your defensive style are applied differently, depending upon whether the source of threat is personal or situational. Some sources of threat are, of course, a mixture of both the situational and the interpersonal.

Such sources of threat that can cause stress and/or conflict in a number of ways are indicated below:

Psychological Threat
- Failure, or the fear of it
- High risk and unfamiliar situations
- Criticism of your performance, personal goals or values

Situational Threat
- Unrealistic deadlines or goals
- Vague objectives
- Increased responsibility for people or projects

Many people find that their behavioral preferences are different when they are under stress. This can often be due to the fact that in functioning under conditions of difficulty and threat we find, often just through trial and error, that a different mix of styles is more effective than the ones we use when things are going well for us.

When we use similar behaviors in both comfortable and stressful situations, it indicates that we have confidence in and value our style mix. If our behaviors are different in comfortable and stressful situations, it is worthwhile to think about why we use our strengths differently and what the implications for our relationships with others might be.

You might ask, "Could I benefit in either favorable or unfavorable conditions if I used more or less of certain strengths?" For most of us, the answer is "Yes." In effect, you may have more options to handle situations than you realize.

On a final note, in LIFO® seminars a full, descriptive report is generated for each participant based on their survey input. For your information we have included two examples of LIFO® Personal Profiles in Appendix I.

LEARNING MORE ABOUT LIFO® PROGRAMS

If at this stage you are interested in finding out more about LIFO® seminars, you will find contact details for the worldwide LIFO® organization in Appendix III. Meanwhile, you will get more of the flavor and depth of the LIFO® philosophy in the chapters that follow.

—

CHAPTER 12

IT IS THE MIX OF YOUR STRENGTHS THAT COUNTS

You now have a good idea of your main strengths based on the LIFO® checklist in the previous chapter. However, there is more to the story than just identifying your strengths – it is the interaction of the four orientations that determines your behavioral tendencies. As in mixing colors, yellow with blue yields a very different result than yellow with red – even when the yellows are of equal intensity. This is also true with Life Orientations®.

Take, for example, John Bellem who has a strong orientation in Controlling-Taking and Supporting-Giving. This represents a combination of decisiveness, activity and direction, along with high ideals, cooperativeness and a willingness to trust others. A colleague Bill Carlton, has just as strong an orientation in Controlling-Taking, but his second strength is in Conserving-Holding (organising, functioning in a systematic and structured way, adhering to policies and procedures, being consistent).

While both are prone to take charge readily, provide direction, and enjoy responsibility, their manner of managing others is different:

John (CT and SG) acts decisively but prefers to involve others in the consideration of issues, using a somewhat "democratic" style of management. His decisions are influenced by long-range objectives, tending to weigh actions against the goals likely to be achieved and their effects on employees. He tends to ask questions about purpose and processes. His process is more informal and intuitive, but once decisions are made he moves rapidly to action steps.

Bill (CT and CH) is a strong manager who emphasizes structure in organizing for tasks. He develops rules and procedures, is clear about bottom-line expectations, and makes decisions primarily on the basis of his own analyses and information. Bill tends to inform others about what to do, how it should be done and when it must be done. He tends to be formal, objective and somewhat distant.

Both want to accomplish a lot, but their differing supporting strengths influence the quality of how things will get accomplished. This interactive influence changes the meaning of the profile.

Now, if we add the Adapting-Dealing strengths of Robert Anthel to his strong Controlling-Taking orientation, the portrait would change again. You would find a highly enthusiastic and friendly manner, a personalized approach to different individuals – a manner that enables him to convince his staff on the values of what he proposes. In contrast to John and Bill, he would be more outgoing, contact staff more frequently, be more quick to praise and encourage. John and Bill would tend to be more task-centered and critical.

These three managers combined various orientations with their Controlling-Taking strength. In the following examples we will examine the combination of different strengths with a strong Supporting-Giving style.

A common type, for example, can be seen in Margaret Talley's profile that contains both Supporting-Giving and Conserving-Holding peaks (SG and CH). She is concerned about doing things well and exactly. She holds little room for error – spending a great deal of energy to assure results as "perfect as they can be." Margaret expends care in planning thoroughly, establishing checkmarks for evaluation, and striving hard until the desired results are obtained. While she involves others and is considerate of their need for guidance, she holds herself and everyone else to the highest standards imaginable – she is a stickler for accuracy.

—

Mary James' profile, on the other hand, concentrates on Supporting-Giving and Adapting-Dealing elements (SG and AD). She is a warm, outgoing person who delights in being as friendly and cooperative as possible. Mary tends to balance criticism with praise. She makes an effort to know people well, to listen carefully and to respond empathetically. It is important for her to feel accepted and to create harmonious relationships.

Now consider a seemingly contradictory combination of Conserving-Holding and Adapting-Dealing orientations that appear in George Jensen's profile (CH and AD). While certainly structured and organized, George is sensitive to reactions and suggestions from others – developing structures that others will feel meets their needs. He makes sure to understand concerns and needs of others and that, in turn, influences him in designing systems. This is in contrast to Bill Carlton (remember he combines CT and CH strengths). George would never insist on imposing structure that others would not accept favorably. Instead, he builds friends and maintains smooth relationships with everyone.

Such combinations work in similar ways when the going gets tough as well (what we called unfavorable conditions earlier). A person with strong Controlling-Taking and Conserving-Holding orientations would be a much more severe opponent than one with Controlling-Taking and Adapting-Dealing. **In fact the key to whether relationships will be productive is the secondary score.** If two "opponents" – each a combination of Controlling-Taking and Conserving-Holding – should fight, they combat hard and vigorously, stubbornly maintaining their positions. Two other "combatants" who each combine Controlling-Taking and Adapting-Dealing styles might fight just as hard, but they would be willing to compromise when they see there is little possibility of convincing the other.

It is important to understand that **you are not necessarily trapped by the combinations of your strengths.** On the contrary, when such combinations contain different, strong behavioral components, they can provide alternative possibilities for your actions. When you become excessively committed to one way of doing things, and things do not go as well for you as you had expected, you might then consider focusing on an alternative strength. A shift to that secondary style can have very positive consequences. So, despite a tendency for spontaneous and immediate action if you are Controlling-Taking, the strong presence of Supporting-Giving might delay your quick response with the first idea that comes into your mind, until you have had a chance to check it out with others. With a secondary strength you have at hand a powerful ally for providing more flexibility.

This possibility is clear when we have a secondary major strength in our arsenal. However, there is some value in even our lesser-used strengths. **Actually, each of us can employ *all* of the orientations sometimes.** This fact has implications for personal change. Someone who rarely uses adapting-dealing behavior is not devoid of that behavior. It's simply that he/she doesn't choose that behavior as the preferred way of dealing with events. All of us have had some experiences where employing a little used behavior has become necessary or valuable for special circumstances. It is not that we don't know how to behave, but simply that we fail to use that behavior often.

As a reminder, behavior is influenced not only by orientations, but also by meanings, needs and roles as well. **Here is a story that illustrates the point:**

In one of our training seminars a manager was revealed to be heavily Controlling-Taking and extremely low in preference for using Adapting-Dealing behaviors. Indeed, his behavior in the seminar highly reflected his profile. He was overly participative, insistent on his opinions, and resisted directions. During the workshop, in addition to the basic LIFO® survey another one that focuses on selling styles was also administered. After the second survey, the entire class was dumbfounded to discover this manager was not only high in Controlling-Taking but also in Adapting-Dealing. When the group expressed their disbelief, he

—

told us that he had been a salesman for many years and knew you could not sell without attending to the customer's feelings and attitudes. Some wit in the class then said, "In that case, have you ever considered treating everyone as customers?!" This remark had a big impact on the manager. Later, during an evening session where he charmed everyone with his good will and musical talent, he explained that he had been influenced by the idea that as a manager one should focus solely on task and direction. This is why he had been so assertive and opinionated in the class. When he had been reminded of his sales experience he realized immediately that he had been failing to pay attention to people's feelings and needs.

If the impacts of your behaviors are not what you expect or hope for, you should first question whether you're interpreting the situation correctly.

Some questions that you might ask yourself when another person responds differently than you expected include the following:

- How did the other person interpret my behavior?
- What did they think about my intentions?
- Am I sensitive to the signals they may be sending?
- Do I understand my own feelings about this issue?
- What is a positive way of viewing their reaction, assuming the best of intentions?
- What can I do to let them know I understand their interpretation and reaction? *How should I act? What should I say?*
- What can I do to change their interpretation so they will view my response more in line with my intention? *Is there congruency between what I mean and what I say or how I act?*

Understanding Congruency

We mentioned earlier that the LIFO® checklist you completed provides a good sense about your preferred style(s) while a complete LIFO® survey offers additional, valuable inputs. With the full survey you not only receive total scores that give you a fuller sense of your preferred, backup, and least used styles – you also get that information broken down between your style preferences in both comfortable (*favorable*) and stressful (*unfavorable*) circumstances.

In addition, you would also receive *sub-scores* that provide very telling measures about how you perceive your *intentions, actual behaviors, and the impact of your behaviors.*

The intention scores reflect what you want to happen and/or you are hoping to happen in the relationship.

The behavior scores reflect how you try to get what you want.

The impact scores provide an indication of how your behavior affects the target of your message.

When these scores are similar the likelihood is that the other person with whom you are communicating sees you as someone who is acting in a congruent manner. In other words, things seem to be consistent – you are easier to understand. There are no mixed messages. So in your communications, the words seem to match the feelings and actions.

If, on the other hand, there are significant differences between the three scores, others may experience you as acting in an incongruent way. Your words, feelings and actions do not seem to match – it may be harder to understand you in those areas. And it may be difficult to build credibility.

Looking more deeply we can see the following:

Intention as it relates to Behavior

- When behavior scores are significantly less than intention scores, it may mean that you lack experi-

---

ence in that area or have not practiced those behaviors enough.

- When behavior scores are greater than intention scores, it may mean that you over rely on certain behavior despite situational differences. It might also mean that you are not fully aware of your own intentions.

Behavior as it relates to Impact

- When impact scores are less than behavior you may be using the wrong behaviors. Or you may be using the correct behaviors, but not using them effectively. Sometimes you may have an idea of appropriate behavior that differs from those conventionally held by others. This can be particularly true in cross-cultural circumstances.

For example, one manager lowers his voice and speaks slower when angry, but his staff and colleagues have difficulty realizing he is angry. Interestingly, sometimes our reputation for a strong orientation in one area may cause our behaviors to be misinterpreted. One woman has very high Controlling-Taking scores. In the Supporting-Giving area her behavior scores are much higher than her impact. It seems that people interpret her helping behavior as controlling, a carryover from her strong CT style. Such a difference may suggest that this is an area for development.

- When impact scores are greater than behavior, either the behavior is very intense indeed or the "reputation" of other score areas is causing the behavior to be misunderstood. One person has very high Conserving-Holding scores. Although his Adapting-Dealing Behavior scores are also high, he does not seem to have much impact. His ordinarily serious and restrained behavior makes it hard to recognize when he is flexible and humorous. For him, it may take more Adapting-Dealing behavior than he feels is necessary to achieve the desired effect.

Intention as it relates to Impact

• When the impact is more than is intended, either you are using more intense behavior than you realize or you are relying on the incorrect behavior to get things done. Things may be different than you realize or you might be underestimating your own intentions.

One company president complained about the fact that his executive staff members, a group of brilliant people, seldom participate in management discussions. Videotapes of meetings revealed that he started discussions by telling how he felt about issues and then solicited comments. He believed he was being open but overlooked the fact that people saw him as the boss telling them what he wants. When he learned to introduce the issue and let his own ideas come last, participation was much livelier.

In a similar instance, despite training and recognition, another chief executive never did change his behavior. Upon interviewing him, it was evident that his real intention was to dominate the group and always remain in control. He underestimated his intention score. He never did succeed in developing more interactions with his staff.

Sometimes our expectations of others influence our behavior. We feel we should use more of a specific behavior because of what people expect or because it seems appropriate to the role. Placed in a new position, one manager was having serious problems with his professional staff. While rating his intention in Controlling-Taking as low, his behavior and impact were very high. This troubled him. Discussions revealed he felt that as a manager he was supposed to show he was in charge all the time.

—

From a practical point of view, if you are getting results from your behaviors that are surprising to you, ask yourself several questions:

- Are there areas in which you need to control or modify your behavior in order to achieve the desired effect?
- Are there areas in which you need to develop more skill in using particular behaviors?
- Are there areas in which you need to be more aware of your impact – to check with others about how they experience your behavior?

Looking Deeper

One further use of the sub-score interpretations from a LIFO® survey is the exploration of the individual's motivation and feelings to a greater depth – a journey to understanding the complexities of dynamic forces underlying behavior. As you look for reasons for the lack of congruency you will learn much more about the forces that influence your behavior.

There is, however, a more obvious use that has practical utility for modifying behavior and feelings. After all, it is behavior that creates impact – this is tangible. For situations such as those dealing with customers and clients it is behavior that makes the difference, especially when congruent with desires to establish good relationships. "I couldn't care less about what you think as long as you treat me decently," said one patient in a dental office.

However, consider the statement, "I felt I didn't mean much to you when you didn't respond to my comment." When questioned, the other person replies, "I'm sorry you felt that way, but I was still reacting to some terrible news I received today – I lost a brother in an accident!" The recipient then usually hurries to say, "I'm sorry – I didn't realize anything like that!" He or she may also add, "I wish you had told me that at the outset!" Clearly our reactions change when we understand the other person's intentions.

One hears statements about someone being well intentioned but inept in what they say or do. If we have such knowledge about the person's intention and understand and accept it as a "good" one, then a lot of behavior may have a different impact. Further, consultants and coaches know that providing feedback about impact enables those with good intentions to modify behavior since as they often say, "I had no idea that you might see it that way!" So, one way of creating change is to either provide feedback or to seek feedback concerning one's behavior and the perception of one's intentions. Getting additional training to utilize your own behaviors more effectively can also be useful.

We also have to recognize that behavioral impact may also be due to our own "selves." For example, someone with a poor self-image might interpret any critical remark as a personal rejection rather than as a difference in view or information. Our reality is, after all, only a subjective one save for agreement about consensual perceptions. In fact, extremely intense reactions that occur may be due to the symbolic triggering of some of our own unconscious memories.

Relationships of trust and long acquaintance provide other contexts that mitigate some of the negative impacts of behavior. They may either allow us to diminish the impact by knowing how that other person tends to react or feel, as well as realize that the temporary reaction does not indicate a permanent change in the relationship. "She always gets angry when she hears something like that!" or "Although that sounded terrible, I can't imagine that she meant to hurt me."

A ground rule might be extended from the implications of the above paragraph, namely, that one should always grant the other person the best of intentions. Providing feedback and checking the actual intention can then determine any more appropriate subsequent reaction. A hostile intention may merit a fight, although it might be interesting to explore further the reason for the hostility. A sharing of the feelings that can ensue and the differing perceptions involved might allow for some problem solving. This should lead to a subsequent change in the relationship. Such an underlying curiosity is what is required for effective relationships and teamwork. This might well be followed up by information about what kinds of behavior might help the "sender" realize their intentions when the impact is not positively received.

The LIFO® Method emphasizes that the awareness of Intention, Behavior and Impact congruency can be used to further all relationships. It stresses the need to seek confirmation and continuous sharing of information whenever there are misunderstandings and negative impacts.

Getting Things Done

You already know that there are many ways to accomplish the same goal. We have also emphasized that in LIFO® terms, there is no one way to achieve success. It is the way in which you use your strengths that will determine your effectiveness. Since people do use different LIFO® styles to achieve the same function, let's take a look at how their behaviors may differ. When reviewing the following table it may be useful to think about the behavior of certain individuals at your office. You should now be able to handle your interactions with them more effectively next time you are working together.

HOW PEOPLE USE DIFFERENT LIFO® ORIENTATIONS TO ACHIEVE THE SAME FUNCTION

SG	CT	CH	AD
HELPING			
• Encourages	• Offers unsolicited advice	• Offers informative and practical advice	• Listens with empathy
• Is non-directive	• Gives prescriptions	• Analyses problems step- by- step	• Helps person to come up with own answers
• Responds to requests	• Insists on his/her help being used	• 'Here are the pros and cons'	• 'What do you want?'
• 'I'm here if you need me'	• 'Here's what I'd do if I were you'		• 'I know someone who can help'
CONTROLLING			
• Sets high standards for others through being needed	• Takes charge and initiates	• Thorough structure, agenda and methods	• Uses finesse and humor
• Does what is right and provides the best advice through group norms	• Uses legitimate authority	• Maintains organizational controls	• Keeps harmony by not revealing own position through relationships
	• Uses direct control	• Documents the position and presents evidence	
ANALYSING			
• Compares against ideal model	• Examines 'bottom line' impact	• Methodically step-by-step	• Examines data for social implications
• Examines for quality	• Selects data to support own position	• Wants the whole story in detail	• Tries for consensus
• Tests for relevancy	• Prefers a quick study	• Organizes data to examine options	• Open to new and conflicting data
			• Uses open-ended approach

—

SG	CT	CH	AD
LEADING			
• Co-operative, participative leadership	•Directive	• Runs a 'tight ship'	• Consensus approach
• Appeals for excellence	• Uses authority	• Thorough policies, procedures and methods	• Tact and flexibility
• Stresses loyalty	• Organizes others to achieve wanted results	• Expert knowledge	• Exercises rational approach
• Group rewards	• Clear objectives		
PLANNING			
• Prefers group planning	• Plans on his or her feet	• In-depth, long range planning	• Concerned over general acceptance of plan
• Long-range vision	• Short-range planning	• Data based	• Assimilates piecemeal effort into creative outcome
• Wants best approach	• Dynamic, quick and informal	• Comprehension of options	• Adapts to external factors as and when they arise
• Delegates with high expectations	• Prominence given to action steps	• 'Build on what we have'	
RISKING			
• Risks public statement of principles	• Risks action rather than delay	• Risks delay rather than action	• Risks being sidelined
• Trusts others	• Forges into untried areas	• Takes risks incrementally	• Places trust in ability to finesse and adapt
• Shares confidences	• Places trust in self	• Trusts data and methods	• Lets others go first
• Accountable to high standards	• Confrontation and visibility		• Trial and error

SG	CT	CH	AD
COMPROMISING			
• Responds to needs of others	• Barters and bargains competitively	• Responds to logic, data and precedent	• Willing to give to get
• Seeks developmental solution	• Split territory solutions	• Compromises to reduce or spread risk if it can be squared with the 'system'	• Keeps actions going
• Wants to do the 'right' thing by everyone	• Responds to appeals of urgency and opportunity		• Gets others to initiate, then adapts
			• Seeks win-win outcomes

CHAPTER 13

STRATEGIES FOR MANAGING YOUR STRENGTHS

How can we make sure that we are using our strengths properly? In this chapter we discuss five strategies for managing your strengths.

One important aspect of the LIFO® concept that sets it apart from other methodologies is that it answers the question, "Now that I have a better understanding of who I am, what can I do about it to modify my behavior?" In the LIFO® method you can work on Strength Management® strategies to change your behavior and improve your effectiveness with others. In this chapter we discuss the five approaches you can begin to use right away.

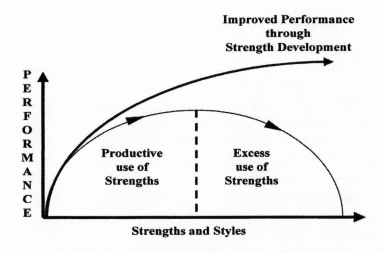

THE LIFO® PERFORMANCE CURVE

1. Capitalize on Your Strengths

We can typically realize more success in our interactions if rely on our best powers (strengths), bringing them to bear when called for and even seeking opportunities to use them. Indeed, there is research that strongly stresses the value of doing just that as contrasted to working on one's weakest strength. Clifton and Paulsen cite a study of specialized reading training for two groups: one with well developed reading skills and another with poor reading skills. An equal amount of special training was provided to the groups. Training exaggerated the differences – the good became superb and the poor became close to average. **The most powerful and easiest strategy available to us depends on capitalizing on our strengths. In effect, we should be trying to take advantage of our best resources.**

The first step to capitalize on your strengths begins with **confirming your strengths:**

The primary goal for use of the LIFO® Survey is to help you identify your strengths. A further developmental goal is to make sure that you have positive feelings about those talents and skills. Evidence exists that the more confident one is about a characteristic, the more one is likely to use it. This self-confidence also gives us the impetus to develop additional skills.

In our seminars we ask people to write positive descriptions of their own behaviors, attitudes and achievements and then speak about them to the rest of the group. Many people feel hesitant to do so, but as they continue to talk they start feeling more confident (in the seminar this activity occurs after people have participated in many activities with each other and have had time to observe one another), especially when they realize others see those strengths in them as well.

The group engages in a *strength-bombardment exercise* where each member takes a turn expressing appreciation of the other's positive traits – of contributions made, pleasant impressions, helpfulness, etc. Admiration and praise flow during this exercise. The effect of this experience is powerful. People feel touched to receive such wonderful treatment and appreciation. The experience is intended to leave everyone with a reservoir of confidence and assurance about their strengths (believing in self) and encouragement to use them whenever there is an opportunity to do so.

When we have an internal image of success or self-confidence it enables us to use that strength with vigor whenever it is needed. Empirical analysis supports this view. For example, Bass and Associates observed that confidence was a major factor in the expression of leadership impact. Crowell, Katcher & Miyamoto found that those who regarded their communicative skills highly were more active and successful communicators.

Use your skills whenever you can. If you are intuitive, trust your judgment and act on it. If you have fine reasoning skills, examine possibilities and provide your recommendations. If you are highly social, help others understand what is happening or volunteer to write letters and work on public relations. In one company, the death of a personnel manager created a huge void. Yet, one engineer who, as a supervisor, had a fine reputation for dealing with his people, volunteered to take over while the company found a new person for the job. In a few weeks, it was evident that he was handling things as well, if not better, than the former personnel manager. The company awarded him the position permanently.

In a small microchip company, a new chip was being developed that required an innovative design which would have implications for a whole new range of products. At the outset, one of the engineers asked whether he could take charge of the new project. Although the company was considering someone else, the assertiveness of the request intrigued the company's President who decided to appoint him as the project manager. He never regretted it. The project was completed on schedule and within budget and the product became the leading moneymaker for the company.

As you can see from the above examples, sometimes it pays to call attention to your skills. Being passive and assuming others will recognize your value and contribution (a Supporting-Giving excess) does not get you noticed. Do not be afraid to let others know about your strengths, but be careful that you do not come across as arrogant (a Controlling-Taking excess).

In a way, capitalising on your strengths is the easiest strategy to employ. It requires little change and is merely the greater use of strengths that you have already developed.

2. Augment Your Strengths

There are times when our strengths do not cover the need of a given situation. Sometimes we must rely on others who can bring different skills to the issue at hand and thereby help us to handle more easily whatever is involved. This does not require any change in your behavior, rather an appreciation of other people's skills and their willingness to employ them. This is precisely the case where "two heads are better than one." A nonsystematic, often casual manner combined with impulsiveness has often led one of the authors to undesired consequences. However, in serious business situations he has learned to augment his own skills by employing attorneys and accountants. They provide the necessary attention to detail required to take care of certain matters.

Augmenting requires, therefore, that you are willing to accept your own skills and appreciate those of others – to feel okay about not being successful in everything – as long as there are others who can help. This leads us to realize that the worst mistake managers can make is to select everyone in their own image. While it may make it more comfortable to deal with everyone in the team, it leaves a terrible vulnerability in the group in those strength areas that are used least. A confident investment group that was emboldened by several aggressive and successful decisions was dominated by principals with high Controlling-Taking orientations. Consequently, they failed to stay close to changing market conditions, didn't analyse market trends, and suffered some severe losses. They later hired managers who could track events in detail, slowing decisions but optimising results.

R. Meredith Belbin, widely respected researcher and author on team-building, has experimental verification of the superiority of team decision making by groups with varied orientations, contrasted with ones who contained those of only one or a few orientations.

3. Extend Your Strengths

There are occasions when you may not be able to use the strengths of others but can begin to build your own arsenal of skills further by learning more about your least used skills and

---

126

practicing them. Impulsive people, for example, can learn to use checklists, schedule events, review expenses, and contact others for opinions before reacting. This is a strategy that requires effort and discipline.

What Is Your Least Used Strength?

What Can You Do To Reduce Your Vulnerability and Increase Your Skills In This Area?

Typically you can extend your strengths in three ways. Firstly, you can choose low-risk situations to practice little used skills. Take a chance and test yourself in practice. Have a go when the stakes are not high and see what it is like to behave in a slightly different manner. Then take a moment to assess the outcome. In the best case try your modified or new behavior with someone whose feedback you value and can trust.

The second way to extend your strengths is to buy a book such as this. Of course, knowledge of a need to develop your strengths is not the same as practicing. Nothing can substitute for going through the actual effort of "doing" in order to get a real time feeling for what it means to behave differently.

Thirdly, there is an enormous selection of seminars on skill improvement from which to choose. These can be very effective, particularly if you attend an interactive, highly participative workshop where you have ample chance to experiment with new behaviors during role-plays and exercises. The following table provides some examples of courses recommended for extending your least used strengths. It also lists some training programs for controlling excessive use of your strengths.

—

SAMPLE STRENGTH MANAGEMENT®
TRAINING PROGRAMS

SUPPORTING/ GIVING	CONTROLLING/ TAKING	CONSERVING/ HOLDING	ADAPTING/ DEALING
Extending Strengths	*Extending Strengths*	*Extending Strengths*	*Extending Strengths*
Customer Service Training Developing Coaching Skills Excellence oriented programs Valuing Diversity Team Building Networking	Leadership Training Confidence Building Exercising Initiative Outward Bound	Time Management Control Systems Decision-making and Problem Solving Analysis and research techniques Organizational frameworks	Negotiating Skills Sensitivity Training Sales Training Creativity Programs Communication Skills Listening Skills
Controlling Excesses	*Controlling Excesses*	*Controlling Excesses*	*Controlling Excesses*
Assertiveness Training	Conflict Management Strategic Thinking Stress Management Time Management Listening Training	Increasing Spontaneity Elements of Risk-Taking Confidence Building	Congruence Training Confrontation Skills Confidence Building

4. Bridge Your Strengths to Another's

If you can determine another person's preferred way of being approached and of handling situations and relationships, you can modify your style mix to that person. Likewise, you can also lead people with whom you work towards *your* preferred orientations so that they can modify their behaviors to allow you to become more productive. Essentially this form of bridging enables each person to meet each other in a way that is acceptable and productive for both.

Experience has demonstrated time and time again that working in teams comprised of people with different styles produces a productive synergy. This reflects what we call *blending of styles between individuals* (as distinct from the blending of styles in your own LIFO® profile). In a productive team we see a willingness to merge orientations into a *new collective style* that takes advantage of all the strengths present. Thus a mixture of Controlling-Taking, Conserving-Holding and Adapting-Dealing may mean that no decision will be made before solid planning has taken place, be practical and within budget, and be likely to receive approval and acceptance by those who will be affected by the decision.

Is there someone with whom you have to work whose style is very different from yours?

How could you bridge your style to work well with that person?

5. Control Excess Uses of Your Strengths

This is the hardest strategy to follow since we overdo things when driven by unconscious factors, like threats, that we sense in situations. Our defences trigger intense responses that may be inappropriate. Encountering resistance from a potential customer, a salesman presses so hard that he drives the customer away. A modest manner causes an administrative assistant to respond immediately to a request because he cannot say no. An accounts manager insists on assiduously following procedures despite the fact he is under severe pressure to come up with an immediate progress report. Asked a question by a critic, a manager provides so lengthy and detailed an answer he bores his audience.

We can help to control such excesses. To do so we need to try a number of approaches. Here are eleven that you might explore.

A. Recognize the impact of your behavior

If you offered help to someone but they reacted as if you had criticized them you'd wonder why, provided of course you noticed their reaction. Pay attention to your audience – if they are not responding as you hoped, if they respond negatively, the chances are you're behaving excessively.

—

B. Ask for feedback

This is an effective way to gain such information. "I feel I'm not reaching you. Can you tell me what I'm doing that makes that happen? What could I do to reach you?" Or, "I value your approval and acceptance, what do I need to do to get it?" or, "How should I have presented this idea to you so that you would accept it?"

C. Alert people to your communication preferences and habits

Sometimes we communicate in ways that might be a "turn off" to others. If we alert people to these inclinations of ours, we help prevent their misunderstanding or misinterpreting our remarks.

Example 1: A South American friend lets people know he tends to express ideas intensely and he reacts loudly if something bothers him. He tells people they should realize he is not expressing anger at them, just letting his feelings out.

Example 2: An attorney warns new acquaintances he has an "occupational hazard" of reacting to new information with questions, pressing people hard to prove their points. He says up front, "sorry, that's simply my way of learning. I'm not trying to make you look foolish."

D. Provide an alternative context for interpretation

In this way the threatening sting of some excesses can be removed so the "audience" can hear the underlying message.

E. Sanction others to let you know when you are overdoing a behavior

This is an excellent method to keep you from heading to a counterproductive outcome.

Example: Team building programs stress the importance of establishing a mutual contract to help each member alert you when you are not up to your best. This can help you gauge reactions and warn you of excesses. In a sales training seminar a "team" of two sales people were observed dealing with a client. If one of the pair were too abstract in his presentation, the other would pat his head; if the other was too detailed, his partner would look at his watch. These were "feedback" signals designed to alert the person speaking that he might not be getting the effect he wanted and he should shift into another mode. And, in one instance where the other person was not heeding the signal, the partner broke into the conversation to make a smooth transition. They had developed a subtle set of signals that could provide continuous feedback about excesses that could allow each to manage his presentation in an effective way.

F. Understand your own reactions

If you are feeling tense, sensing you're under severe strain and working awfully hard to make a point, your behavior may be signalling this to others. You can practice being your own observer for such signals. People tend to emit warning signs to themselves, but until you are sensitized to them you may not pick them up. The following chart provides examples of what may be typical early warning signals for certain behaviors within the four LIFO® styles.

STYLE	STRENGTHS	EARLY WARNING	EXCESSES
Supporting-Giving	Considerate	Overly helpful	Self denying
Controlling-Taking	Confident	Cocky	Arrogant
Conserving-Holding	Thorough	Elaborate	Pedantic
Adapting-Dealing	Flexible	Vacillating	Inconsistent

—

G. Stop the ongoing behavior

A common reaction for many people is to persist when frustrated, to defend intensely when attacked. You may find it useful to listen to your feelings, stop the behavior and see if there is an alternative approach that can be used. Stopping might involve a request for a temporary break, such as when negotiators take a recess when reaching a deadlock, so you can cut the behavior off. You may also find it useful to acknowledge your own feelings and explore the rationale for the other person's reactions to your behavior.

Example 1: When we visited one of the managers who had attended a recent seminar we saw a plaque on his desk. Written in bold letters was the statement: "YOU DON'T HAVE TO RESPOND NOW!" He found that an effective reminder to control his impulsivity.

Example 2: One of the authors used to keep a small paper in his top drawer with the letter "P" written on it. When situations became highly tense and pressurized he would look at the "P" to remind him to regain a sense of "Perspective" on the situation at hand.

H. Explore alternatives

Are you sure the other person meant to be critical? Does the fact the boss offered so much explanation really mean he thought you lacked brains, or was he trying to help because so much rode on this situation? When someone barged into your office and asked you to do something for them, were they rude or just overly concerned about something at the moment? How you interpret the situation influences your response, especially if it seems threatening.

Kenneth Finn has developed a therapeutic model called "Recharacterization Therapy" that consists of having people try to reframe their views of what is happening. By changing one's interpretation – putting a more positive cast or a longer-range view – things can appear quite different. The new perspective may enable you to bring a more productive response to bear on the situation.

Example: Invited to take a scenic tour of Chicago in a small private plane, one of the authors was panicked by every bit of turbulence the plane encountered, pleading with the pilot to return to the airport. He calmed down when the pilot said, "These are only bumps in the air road, think of them as bumps you run into in a car!" This was enough to change the whole experience, not only for that flight, but also for any other times when a plane is rocked by rough air.

A bit of humor can help too – what is funny about what is happening? Since we often tend to think of things from our own point of view, how might it seem to the other person? What would happen if we would extend the benefit of the doubt to the other person, if we did not have to be right about everything?

I. Avoid the situations that push you into excessive behavior

If you are always out of control in some situations and cannot handle the fears and stress, consider staying out of them. Either delegate these cases to others or refrain from the encounter.

Example 1: An engineer has a friend with a sailboat. This friend generously invites him for day excursions. On the first one he was anxious whenever the boat heeled and also felt a little seasick. He forced himself to go several times more (he did not want to be unappreciative) but never felt comfortable. Finally he decided not to accept any more invitations. "I really don't see the sense of making myself anxious and calling it pleasure!"

Example 2: A distinguished and highly experienced marketing manager could never make a decent presentation to the Board of Directors. He would hem and haw, fumble over words, talk in a low voice and generally make a mess of it. Finally, he designated one of his assistants to be the department's presenter. He would assist by answering questions or providing additional information (activities which he could always handle) but never again made a speech.

J. Further Training Courses

Pursue a training program that may help you deal with excessive use of your strength (see the table in this chapter)

K. Counselling and Therapy

There are times when we find ourselves unable to cope: maybe behaving out of control or in ways that do not represent us well to others. If these feelings and behaviors persist and the various strength management® strategies cannot help, it may be time to get some professional help. Psychological counselors and therapists provide help in understanding the feelings involved that elicit inappropriate behaviors. They help you explore possibilities for changing your ability to deal with difficult people and events. Even at emotional low points it is possible to realize more potential for improving your outlook on life and work than you could have ever thought possible.

CHAPTER 14

THE LIFO® APPROACH TO TIME MANAGEMENT

If you ask any working person what his or her biggest need is, you will invariably get the reply, "More time!" The fact is, no matter how we try to deal with all the things we do, time is finite. You cannot expand time, you cannot change time – if you want to be more productive you must use the time that you have more effectively.

As you might expect, how you experience time is influenced by your style. Each of us has a different response to questions such as the following:

- When do I feel that time is well spent?
- What is an enjoyable time for me?
- What types of activities do I find most satisfying? Dissatisfying?
- When does time drag on for me?

Looking at our different preferred styles we can see that how we use time or are affected by it may vary. Now that you know your LIFO® orientations, how do the following descriptions fit your perceptions and use of time?

Supporting-Giving

For you time is most exciting and meaningful when devoted to projects of significance, when participation is encouraged and requested by others, when there are opportunities to give advice and be of assistance to people, and when you can live up to your own ideals. Indeed, a statement such as, "I/we would like your help," is a powerful and almost compulsively attractive invitation for you to invest time with others.

While everyone experiences pleasure in pursuing matters of interest and importance, for the Supporting-Giving style time seems generated by the demands of others and the responsibilities of one's roles as manager, employer, parent, teacher or child. From this perspective you do not feel that you are the master of your own time. While goals may be clear, you do not use them to establish time priorities and control the flow of events accordingly. Thus, despite the best intentions, you may not be able to use any of the techniques advocated by time management experts. It is very common for you forget to reserve time for yourself. You usually think of others first and expect others to be considerate of your time.

Learning to value yourself is the key — something that is more likely to be obtained from assertion training experiences than in time management courses. People who feel guilty do not feel their time is their own — if someone *asks* them for something, they drop what they're doing and try to give the other person what is wanted. If you are an employee like this, you will never have enough time to do your own work.

Controlling-Taking

A rapid pace, challenging events, variety and opportunities for making things happen are most satisfying for you. Mastering skills, dealing with problems no one else can solve, and risk-taking all provide other important satisfactions. Time drags for you when nothing is happening or you experience long delays. For example, we know a Controlling-Taking individual who has been accepted in a position with a firm that does work in the United States military defence field. Typically security clearances are required before an employee can actually start working in such jobs. The period after his hiring and before his clearance was granted was terribly trying for this person.

For a Controlling-Taking person time is experienced as urgent. If you wish to do something, you want to do it *now*. Taking time to simply think about issues when something needs to be done is distressing since the built-up tension cannot be discharged. Distractions during slack periods can become compelling. Focusing is difficult to sustain for long periods, especially if repetition causes you to lose interest or you try to perform mechanically while you are preoccupied with other things.

You enjoy mastering new skills. Learning new things can become an end in itself and possibly lead to change. Problem solving by yourself provides a lot of fun.

The time management problems that you have as Controlling-Taking are often due to your confidence that you can handle a lot of things, thus fueling your tendency to take on too much. Simply imposing a scheduled system that is highly structured is not likely to alleviate these problems. It is like the story of the man told to count to ten before reacting to threats. After considerable effort and practice, he encountered his next challenge, got to the count of three before he said, "To hell with it! I'm going to jump in with both feet!" Redirecting activity from direct "doing," delegating more, working with others to establish plans and reviews can provide some assistance. Structuring your encounters with others in order to reduce demands on you and provide protective barriers can also help. In one company, the president literally had an extra wall built to hide his office because people would simply walk in and he would feel bound to respond immediately. To cope with this tendency that seriously affected his effective use of time, he also found it necessary to change his secretary from a warm, friendly person to one who was cordial but firm. While his general action patterns remained the same, the barriers that were established enabled him to get more effectively use of his time at the office.

—

For Controlling-Taking styles putting bounds on activities so that they provide smaller and regular units of accomplishment also helps to sustain focused interest in what is happening.

Long projects with poorly developed milestones do not work comfortably with this style. You can become distracted too easily by more novel and interesting events. If you really want to motivate someone with this style, as a last resort, you could tell him or her that, "No one else has ever been able to complete a project like this!"

Conserving-Holding

For the Conserving-Holding person to feel right about work there has to be enough time provided to do a job right. Organizing activity, planning the processes and schedules, checking things carefully, following well-established and tested procedures and working within prescribed boundaries afford the most pleasurable uses of time for you. Additional satisfaction will be derived from opportunities to analyse and research issues, to explore systematically possible outcomes and to discuss reasons and facts in a sound and rational manner.

When time is rushed or when there is no definitive task structure those who favor the Conserving-Holding style will feel time is very heavy. Those of you who fit this category are likely to feel uncertain and anxious. You will probably spend time in questioning others until either the time limits are extended or the situation has been defined more clearly. Gradual conditioning may help you deal with uncomfortable circumstances. Working within intervals that are a little shorter than usual and/or diminishing periods until a more rapid pace of activity occurs might also help. This may not work, however, if you are heavily entrenched in this style.

In one company a highly skilled manager of a market research group was offered a promotion to the position of marketing director. He refused the promotion, a perplexing decision to top management who felt he should have been grateful for the opportunity to advance his career. Yet the manager himself felt the pace and demand would not permit him to function at the level of excellence he desired – that he would be buffeted by pressures forcing him to provide swift responses.

Sometimes, if you are managing someone with this style, you can help her by providing a structure that alleviates some of the perceived risk associated with the short time responses that are required. You can tell such a person that you know the answer will be incomplete or less than perfect – that all you want is a statement of position and recommendation by a particular time.

Adapting-Dealing

If this style is yours, you are likely to enjoy most those times that you can spend with people. You need to be up and around, contacting others, exchanging pleasantries, gathering information from informal talks, and sensing what people are feeling about various things. The chances to meet new people, to arrange important events, and to negotiate matters provide the highlights of each day and offer the most fun for you.

Detailed planning, repetitive work, periods of long absence from friends and acquaintances, and highly scheduled work are somewhat distasteful to you. As a result, time can be eroded by your need to socialize. You cannot simply accept the lessons of time management. They may allow you to use time more productively, but they would take the excitement and interest out of working.

Pairing with others who are more disciplined yet friendly, and choosing work where opportunities exist for receiving high visibility can help. Positive feedback and encouragement for trying new behavior would also be important in motivating you to manage time more effectively.

Some Self-help Exercises on Time Management

Take a look at the chart below (originally developed by Kenneth Finn of The Gemini Corporation). It summarizes how each of the four LIFO® orientations relate to time. Then answer the two questions at the bottom of the page.

1. Refer back to your most preferred and back-up styles. After reviewing the information for them in the above chart, what are the two factors that have the greatest **negative** impact on your use of time?
2. Now, try to think of some specific situations that you will face in the near term. Using what you know about your preferred styles, what actions can you take to use time more efficiently?

	Supporting-Giving	Controlling-Taking	Conserving-Holding	Adapting-Dealing
Time Strengths	Working with others	Covering many tasks	Analyzing and getting facts	Trying new things
	Helping and assuring	Generating new approaches	In-depth study of problems	Resolving conflicts
	Doing what is relevant and best	Urging for closure on projects	Methodical and systematic	Finding ways around difficulties
Time Binds	Saying yes to too many people	Doing too many different things	Overly analytical	Waiting for others to lead off
	Trying for perfection	Everything is urgent	Being too cautious	Always open to others
	Pursuing impractical ideals	Acting impetuously	Minimizing risks	Overly flexible
Time Leaks	Rescuing everybody else	Putting out fires	Over-elaborate reports	Abrupt changes in direction
	Critical of self and others	Jumping from task to task	Continuing discussions	No visible plans
Personal Fears	Feeling depressed over unfulfilled	Projects at various stages of completion	Holding things up for more facts and figures	Many possibilities, ideas
	Missing a chance to be helpful	Losing an opportunity	Not understanding the situation	Loss of approval
	Not being able to do my very best	Not appearing competent	Not being comprehensive and complete	Too much disagreement
To Save Time	SET LIMITS	GET FOCUSED	GET GOING	GO FIRST
	e.g., closed door policy	e.g., key in on a few tasks	e.g., think of doing	e.g., stay with it

141

A further suggestion about improving your Time Management

As you advance up the hierarchy in your career, you begin to *do* certain tasks less while you learn to *supervise* **others** who are doing. You start to become judged on the collective output of units and teams that report to you. While your technical job skills may still be important, you have to develop new skills and areas of knowledge that will enable you to coach your staff members to achieve common goals. You must move on to do new things, perhaps at a more strategic level, while still ensuring that day-to-day business gets done. **One vital skill that is often underestimated in order to accomplish this transition efficiently is the ability to *delegate* work.**

It is often thought that the main reason to delegate is to move work off of your desk and onto another's desk, so you can be freed up to undertake other tasks. While this may in fact happen, there is another valuable purpose for delegating.

Delegation is a way in which we can development the knowledge and skills of people who work for us. The experience takes place on the job where learning for the individual can be maximized and the company can benefit at the same time. In addition, delegation can be an effective confidence builder as your employees learn to take on and succeed in new tasks.

There are a few key steps that you should follow in all situations where delegation is being done. They are preparation, briefing the employee, and follow-up. An understanding of the employee's LIFO® orientations can assist you in all three steps.

1. Preparation

First you should clarify and prioritize what needs to be done. When starting the day many managers find it useful to make a list of the key tasks that need to be accomplished. Some even create the list as their last task the day before. This way, they can get started right away in the morning. You need to decide what you must do personally. Clearly, there are tasks that might require your expertise and experience, or some may be of a more confidential nature than others. From the list of things to do determine what can be delegated.

The next step is to match a task to an employee. Ask yourself who has the capability to do this? Who might be able to use this task as a growth experience to learn a new skill or a new area of the business?

Thinking back to your employees' orientations:

Can Bill use his existing strengths to get this work done and in the process become even more productive (i.e., *capitalising* in our LIFO Strength Development® terminology).

Is this a chance to team Jane up with someone else who has strengths she does not have? Jane can be advised to recognize these in her colleague so that she can *augment* her own strengths and become more effective.

Does Bob need an opportunity to practice a strength that he does not seem to use very often? Maybe he can be assigned a task in a low-risk situation to practice a least preferred orientation thereby *extending* his strengths options.

Alternatively, can Sarah use this chance to learn to modify her style mix to others on the assignment, *bridging*, in order to complete the work?

2. Briefing the Employee

Perhaps the most important element to ensure successful delegating is providing the employee with a clear briefing at the outset. Here are some helpful steps to keep in mind.

1. Give the background to the task. It is much more interesting to work on something if we understand at least a little of what it is about.

—

2. Explain how the task fits into a larger scheme of things. Again, we all like to feel part of the bigger picture and a few words of explanation can go a long way to make the task more meaningful. It may also enable the employee to be more creative in solving problems that may exist.

3. Be clear about deadlines. If the employee knows something about the larger picture, where this tasks fits into the whole, there should be no need for discussion of why certain deadlines must be met.

4. Comment on any specific procedures or methodologies that should be followed. There is nothing more demoralising than to work on something only to find out after it is complete that you should have been doing it in another way.

5. Discuss how you will measure successful performance of the task. Here is a good place to emphasize quality of output versus time and effort that is input.

6. How much authority are you granting this individual? Can he make some decisions on his own or must he check back with you?

7. How do you want results to be conveyed? A memorandum? Email? Oral Report?

8. *The LIFO® element of the discussion relates to why you are giving this assignment to the individual in the first place. What do you expect her to be able to learn from it? Using the language of LIFO® orientations and strength development® options makes it easy to convey this information.*

Before finishing you should check for the employee's understanding of the task, his agreement to take it on, and if appropriate, his commitment to completing it successfully. Finally, clarify when you should be involved in the work.

—

3. Follow-up

Make sure you build in a reporting or monitoring system that keeps you informed about progress on the task and the final result. You will find that there are varying degrees of control you will require depending on the person, the task, and the risk of the situation. Your understanding of the employee's styles might also give you some clues about what to expect and how you should handle this aspect of the process. For example, your Conserving-Holding employee might be counted on to provide methodical reports undertaken with due care; whereas, your Controlling-Taking staff member might have a mind to run the assigned project on his or her own terms.

Finally, once all of the above steps have been accomplished, you must release control. Often this is the toughest part of the whole process.

You should keep in mind that the learnings that are gained by delegating do not only flow from you to the employee. You will also learn a great deal about yourself. Keep in mind your own strengths and areas that need further development. By delegating you will certainly encounter different situations that require you to adjust your behavior and communication style in order to achieve a successful conclusion.

CHAPTER 15

CREATING EFFECTIVE TEAMS
THE LIFO® WAY

Teamwork has been a fundamental value throughout humankind's endeavours whether related to hunting and gathering, military matters, sports, or work. In today's business environment teamwork has become even more crucial as no one individual or no one firm can provide all the inputs needed to satisfy an ever-demanding customer.

Teams are formed within your own work unit and increasingly, cross-functionally across other areas in your company. Teams are also being formed with individuals outside your company – suppliers, service providers, and other business partners – in order to meet demands of an increasingly complex world.

Each of us is affected by our team membership, whether we are team leaders or participants. As a manager (team leader) one of your key tasks is to promote team attitudes that lead to achieving results. To do so you must be cognizant not only of performing your own job but how the tasks of each individual on your team relate to the work and concerns of others. In a team environment we are all responsible for the achievement of common objectives. All of the team members must identify with the group goals and hold each other mutually accountable for contributions and achievements in a truly shared sense.

What is a Team?

The term "team" is often used in a way that hides the essential meaning of the word. It becomes a designated way of describing a work group. However, unless a work group requires interdependent functioning *to accomplish* shared goals *it is not a team.*

Effective teams, therefore, are characterized by such attitudes as "we" versus "I," willing contributions, respect for and interest in each other's ideas, support for each other when needed, shared management of responsibilities and continuous evaluation of progress toward goals where member's roles and performance become redefined by circumstances. Team members perform with pride because membership requires their interdependent efforts.

LIFO® Team Benefits

The LIFO® Method enhances such efforts by providing frameworks for understanding and appreciating the unique strengths each team member brings to the group's work. It focuses group problem solving on using these strengths by minimizing defensiveness, focusing on realistic expectations, and providing means of managing conflict and inspiring creativity. Two key concepts, the **strength-weakness paradox** and **strength management,** guide our thinking about team management.

The Strength-Weakness Paradox and Teams

We mentioned earlier that strengths could be viewed as a continuum from strength to weakness – from an under-use to overuse of strengths. As team members we have to know how and why we can rely on each other and we need the time to know each other to get this knowledge. The "non-productive" time that each team spends introducing members to one another, getting acquainted, and objectively debriefing how each member contributes to the team effort provides such knowledge – indeed provides the primary information that ensures we can work together. Actual work sessions, especially following constructive debriefings, give us practical understandings that help us know what to expect from each other.

In time, we discover each other's strong points, what we can count on from each other – where to turn when we need knowledge and skills we lack. We also unearth each other's excesses – overuse of strengths. John may provide excellent descriptions of the background factors affecting our problems, Joe can be counted on to ask searching questions concerning information and help us see the pros and cons of proposals. Beth may energize us to act in a timely way. Robert may be skilled in creating a cohesive climate for discussion. We also find out that John may talk too much about a favored point, and Joe will take too much time analyzing every detail. Beth may be prone to just jumping on the first good idea. And Robert may be focusing on social matters more than is practical.

As we work together we also find signs of other inadequacies – John may not respond swiftly enough to issues, Joe may not consider feelings about issues, Beth may not pay attention to details, and Robert may not respond readily to requests for help.

In good teams, we accept the good along with the bad. As Belbin states in his book, *Team Roles at Work*, we see the aforementioned descriptions of weaknesses as allowable differences and take them into account – and compensate for them. In bad teams, we discover there are destructive behaviors that are not allowable – where personal agendas work against the group objectives. These are a consequence of non-team oriented intentions and would not be sanctioned in an effective team.

Indeed, in their studies of teams Belbin and Hayden discovered that "the best results have come from teams which developed well-informed self-insight and which took appropriate action in managing their style of operation . . . the best team members . . . in one team, recognized that they had a strong preference for both action and autonomy. They therefore decidedd to act independently but in a concerted way in the discharge of their duties . . . ."

Belbin and Hayden further note that "There were many other mechanisms and compensations that teams adopted to overcome a basic weakness. But those adjustments first needed to be triggered off by an awareness of the collective self-image and a desire to manage what was there effectively. A coherent self-image emerged, therefore, not only as an advantage for the progression of individuals but for the team itself. If a team fails to see itself as though from the outside, it cannot use its internal resources or regulate its activities efficiently."

These experiences mirror our own in studies of more than 100 decision-making teams striving to decide which of several candidates would make the best CEO for a company. We found, to quote Belbin again, that "the mature team will cherish whatever abilities it possesses, even those of no more than average order. But because these abilities are used to full advantage, it will achieve superior results.

Inventorying a Team's Strengths and Weaknesses

It is thus critical to create such a shared inventory of team strengths and weaknesses. The LIFO® Survey provides a concrete and objective basis for doing this. Examining the profiles of each of the team members, checking them against group work experiences, *appreciating the strengths*, and *accepting the allowable inadequacies*, team members can readily develop the shared understanding that will help them to use each other's strengths synergistically and to compensate for the skills that are lacking.

Getting Teams in Tune

So, how do we get our teams to function productively? We have found the metaphor of an orchestra instructive and use it to get teams in tune. The following is based on an article, Getting Your Team In Tune, written by Atkins and Katcher, cited in the bibliography.

As we have seen earlier "Do unto others as you would have others do unto you," may be an important moral precept, but it is not necessarily a valuable approach if you are trying to improve your relationships with others and build teams. It presumes that everyone is the same and will respond to identical treatment – being treated the same way you would like to be treated. However, many of the people working for you are not like you. What's more, they are not even like each other. You have to help them relate to each other by teaching them to appreciate other people's styles, strengths and motivations.

To continue to use our musical theme, each of us marches to a different drummer. The secret of good teamwork is blending contrasting styles. If you have the opportunity to build your own team from the beginning you have an excellent chance to succeed, particularly if you know and understand the styles of individuals from whom you can choose. Then you can create the right blend of people. However, we do not often have the luxury to select all or even some of our team members.

To get the best performance from your team you have to get each to give his or her best as individuals while also helping them to build their strengths for peak performance as a group. To achieve this, you must analyse their different styles of operating.

You have learned that people whose dominant orientation is *Supporting-Giving* tend to be trusting, responsive, idealistic and loyal. They try to do the very best they can whenever you assign them a task and they set high standards for themselves and their people. Highly receptive to other's ideas, they co-operate and are helpful, natural team players.

When *Controlling-Taking* is the major orientation, people are openly competitive. They act quickly, express their self-confidence, are persuasive and very competitive. As 'take charge' people they want little, if any, regular supervision. They tell you what needs to be done.

Then there is the *Conserving-Holding* style in which people are methodical and precise. Before they act, they analyse various ways of doing a job. They are thorough and practical, making the most of their existing resources. Often seeming reserved and even unenthusiastic, they nonetheless do a predictable, efficient job.

Finally, those whose dominant style is *Adapting-Dealing* are flexible, enthusiastic and tactful. They never seem to make enemies, charming everyone. They are sensitive to what people want and feel and modify their approach accordingly. Popularity and the spotlight are important to them, but they are open to new ideas and excite fellow workers or subordinates to do the job at hand.

Leading on from this analysis, the following chart provides a summary of all the LIFO® styles with respect to the roles they play in teams. SGs are facilitators, CTs are directors, CHs coordinate, and ADs broker.

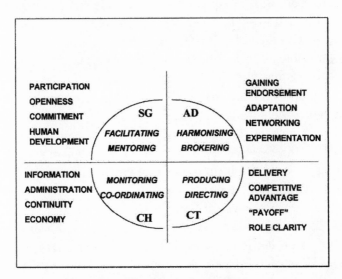

LIFO® TEAM ROLES

Orchestrating Effective Teamwork

Each LIFO® style, with its own unique way of performing tasks, has its role to play within any operating unit. You have to assess each individual's main orientation and gear your mode of **behavior** accordingly. With the different styles as a backdrop you can **understand** how each one makes its special valid contribution to the team's efforts. Team members can learn to appreciate and build on one another's differences by mixing and meshing their styles to achieve maximum team performance overall.

Often, however, such differences are not appreciated because people exaggerate their strengths. They overdo a good thing, pressing a valid orientation across a threshold at which their key strengths become weaknesses.

So, the bossy type, whose usual Controlling-Taking orientation is characterized by initiative and confidence, can become impulsive and arrogant. A carefully methodical and analytical colleague whose orientation is Conserving-Holding becomes plodding, nitpicking and locked into "analysis paralysis." Someone on your team with a Supporting-Giving style can push trust to gullibility and extend concern for excellence to perfectionism. Another with the Adapting-Dealing orientation can exaggerate flexibility into inconsistency and pass from being tactful into being obsequious.

We have seen that frequently people find themselves doing too much of their own good thing simply because their style gives them so much satisfaction and reward. It has made them successful so far, so why not use more of it, even though the situation may not call for it. In the eyes of others this excess seems unnecessary, selfish and frustrating.

Excess can also result from stress in the working environment. Tasks that need to be performed by teams can cause particularly high levels of stress. For instance, objectives may be vague or various members of the team have differing views of what the objectives are. Or perhaps the team has been given what seem like, or are in fact, unrealistic deadlines. Another cause for stress can be that the lines of authority and responsibility are unclear. Team members may not be sure of what they are supposed to be doing and for whom.

Perhaps there are conflicting expectations. A divisional manager may press members of his staff to be more expansive in their marketing efforts but the financial director wants them to watch their costs. Overload is another factor. It occurs when the amount of work is too great and/or those sharing responsibility are too few. It also happens when someone, or even a whole group are in over their heads because of inexperience.

So, team leaders and members have to scrutinize the work environment including its rules and its regulations to see how these affect the team. Such scrutiny may even include examining how people are being compensated if much of their work output depends on team activities. **If you are a team manager** it would be up to you to make appropriate adjustments where necessary and possible, in order to create a workplace that is conducive to teamwork **or, alternatively, for the team to make a positive proposal for the consideration of higher management.**

Getting the Most out of Each Instrumentalist (Team Member)

LIFO® thinking can help a manager find the most effective ways to motivate an employee to complete a task. In the context of working in teams the manager must analyse the styles of the individual team members and then influence them accordingly. This does not mean you have to change your own natural style of managing. What you have to do is find the right motivation and meaning for each person in each position, honour it, and relate to it.

Anyone who has played on a sports team under a good coach or played a musical instrument in a band led by a good conductor can relate to examples when that team leader "pressed the

—

right buttons" to get a teammate to perform better. You will have noticed that the approach used was probably different for different people on the team. Intuitively, the team leader was following the same process – assessing the behavior (style) of the individual and using selective influencing approaches to guide or push the person to achieve better performance.

Playing in Harmony

The work environment has to be constantly surveyed for causes of stress and to attempt to eliminate or reduce these where possible. We tend to look to managers to do that but effective teams share that responsibility and adjust accordingly. In building teams the four LIFO® styles can be reviewed with each individual and at group meetings, emphasizing how to interact to achieve maximum effectiveness. Each person would have a chance to analyse his or her own style. Most people will readily recognize themselves at the group meetings and discussions can center on how the styles interrelate and supplement each other to create teamwork.

There should be an emphasis on the fact that there are no good or bad styles. Once this is understood, the emotional aspect of misunderstandings within a team is defused. Ann, for example, will come to realize that Ted is not a nitpicking obstructionist, that his dominant approach is Conserving-Holding and that people with that profile can use their strengths to make their own particular contribution to the success of the team. If team members understand their own dominant orientation and those of the people about them, they are halfway toward accommodating their behavior with the others and blending their styles.

An important lesson is the discovery that certain individuals can function more effectively in particular roles – sometimes different roles than the ones they have been originally assigned. From a team perspective, the issue is how we can best make use of strengths rather than occupy a particular role. Flexibility then allows us to choose appropriate roles based on strengths. It would be a mistake for example, to assign a major research responsibility to one who does not emphasize a conserving-holding approach in his/her style – or to expect some member to sell ideas to others who lacks strength in the adapting-dealing dimension.

Thus the mixing and meshing of styles can be aided by shifting departmental assignments. The person who hates planning and detail work but loves action could be given a troubleshooter's assignment. Maybe the person who thrives on procedural work should keep the team's minutes and records. (From this perspective, the CEO's of many large companies might even move their most senior managers to new and different jobs on a regular basis. Certainly, this serves as development of senior executives who must gain a broad picture of the business. But it also can play a personal learning role by challenging those executives to blend their own styles across diverse workplaces and working types within the company).

Perhaps, if you are a boss who does not enjoy the coaching side of your responsibilities, you might find a team member whose major orientation is Supporting-Giving. Make him or her your assistant to supplement you in dealing with the development of others.

Similarly, you can use operating style as a criterion when assigning people to team projects. Thus the person who is abrasive and sometimes rubs people the wrong way might be matched with a person whose dominant orientation is Adapting-Dealing. Or the sales person who is great at getting along with customers but is not so hot at organizing could be teamed with someone whose style is dominated by the Conserving-Holding style.

Above all, one has to keep in mind that this is not a one-shot exercise. Periodic meetings need to be set up with a team to review how all members' styles are meshing to achieve departmental objectives and to see when adjustments are needed. That does not mean aimless mutual analysis and name calling, but goal oriented reviews.

Start with any problems that have arisen. Have deadlines been met? Have defects been reduced as planned? What is causing stress? Can we overcome them or do we have to learn to live with them? Team meetings should begin with the work content addressed in this way and as problems are discussed, gradually move into the stylistic aspects of the issues – when problems are not being solved.

Some people object to the idea of discussing their associates' styles because they feel this entails playing amateur psychologist as though this were some form of group therapy. But the fact is that we all do play amateur psychologist, usually at the water-cooler, analyzing why fellow workers and bosses do things.

What is most productive is to get this type of talk out in the open, with a mutually agreed upon and understood set of terms – the four LIFO® orientations – so everyone can benefit from shared insights. As long as we all understand that there are no good or bad styles and that each style makes its special contribution, everyone should be able to view the subject objectively. Therapy is not needed because no one is being blamed and all approaches are valued.

It is essentially a matter of you and the others coming to appreciate more deeply the fact that everyone behaves differently and that there are predictable guidelines for dealing with those differences. They all contribute to achieving the goal of making the beautiful music of peak performance.

Working in Remote or Virtual Teams

We could not complete this chapter without some words about virtual teams and the role that LIFO® methods might play to assist in their development and effectiveness. The development of telecommunications technology and the Internet makes it possible for groups to cooperate in problem-solving modes without direct presence. By logging on, team members can work together or separately on a common task. The effect is close to that of a normal group discussion when working simultaneously via chat software – save for the restrictions of lack of awareness of visual cues (and this, too, can be eliminated by video conferencing techniques).

There are advantages and disadvantages to this technology. Some of these are listed below.

Advantages of Virtual Teamwork

1. The Internet makes it possible to have meetings regularly. Previously, a team that was widely dispersed geographically, communicating via telephone, would have faced difficulties in scheduling, conducting, and coordinating meetings.

2. Internet discussions have the advantage of retaining what everyone has "said" so that all of the input material can be saved for summaries and later review.

3. Ordinarily no one can pay equal attention to all that is being said and done. Since everyone can have complete access to all statements and review them at a later date, this difficulty is alleviated.

4. Discussion can proceed in more orderly fashion, without interruptions.

5. There is more freedom to participate since some of the ordinary psychological restrictions of visual cues are removed.

6. Side conversations can take place without total involvement or consuming the group time.

7. By writing comments, relevance is more apparent. People may think first before replying. A rapid transmission of information is possible, along with speedier decisions.

Disadvantages of Virtual Teamwork

1. Spontaneity is curbed – immediacy of response is modified or halted.
2. Even with video camera, there is a loss of visual cues that exist in the real life group discussions.
3. The human contact of traditional teamwork encourages more identification and builds commitment more rapidly – also encourages understanding and may moderate extreme views.
4. Frustrations can occur when immediate reactions are ignored as others make their own personal statements. (This can happen in a regular discussion but can be controlled more readily by a good process leader. If protocols are established prior to Internet discussion, a similar control can be achieved.)
5. Members have to learn how to use appropriate software, develop new group interaction techniques, and disciplined ways of reviewing and processing information.

The LIFO® Method can be a major aid to overcoming some of the disadvantages experienced by virtual teams by establishing expectations of how the remote workgroup process can affect each individual's style and vice versa. It can also offer clues to small changes in the process that can make it more meaningful to the group as a whole.

By sharing your LIFO® styles with other team members, it is possible to realize the biases and values likely to be emphasized by different people. Team members can recognize how to help each other manage excesses and defensive reactions.

Research into this area is as new as the technology, but here are some typical behaviors that might result from different LIFO® orientations participating in email discussions and Internet workgroups.

—

Supporting-Giving Behavior on a Virtual Team

- Reluctance to participate unless invited by others
- Making many value oriented statements – often of a critical nature
- Seeking guidance and direction
- Allowing more forceful comments because of the anonymity that would not ordinarily exist under ordinary conditions
- Being more sensitive to criticism since everything is written and can be seen by all of the team members (and preserved!)
- Offering too much content in a desire to help

Controlling-Taking Behavior on a Virtual Team

- Becoming excited about the possibility of getting the team together on short notice and have everyone participate. The speed at which problems can be solved and information shared would greatly excite someone who emphasizes this style.
- Becoming frustrated with the pace due to such constraints as protocol and topic focus
- Failure to follow through on a discussion of immediate concerns – not being able to influence a group as quickly as would be the case in face-to-face situations.
- Over participation with many comments and suggestions, not allowing others to respond or giving time for everyone to think about the issues.
- Boredom if process takes too long – may opt to do other things and review material later.
- Desires material with emphases, terseness, editorials rather than long discussions
- Desires changes of pace – may feel that new opportunities may be lost because of the linear nature of the

group process. The CT would like to be working on several things at once but cannot because of the format.

Conserving-Holding Behavior on a Virtual Team

- Prefers organized presentation, highly controlled flow of discussion, and little rambling. The gratuitous comments and similes that punctuate a normal discussion group to add emphasis would take away from a CH natural interest in this way of working.
- Likes to have information arrayed in tables or diagrams. Sometimes this is possible with a 'whiteboard' type of software but if the system is text only, the process may be more confusing for an advocate of this style.
- Prefers logical structure – may be annoyed by lack of clear-cut directions. Setting limits on when general comments are appropriate and when creative brainstorming is needed would make it easier for the CH.
- Wants discussions in length and time to study (either pre-E-mailed or time deferrals of decisions). Breaking the process up to have an information input session; followed later by a problem-solving portion would give the CH time to think.
- Can enjoy the process of learning procedures, protocols etc.

Adapting-Dealing Behavior on a Virtual Team

- Enjoys variety and playfulness that can be found in a normal on-line discussion where many of the status barriers are removed and people feel freer to participate. This would be exciting to someone who relies on this style since it gives the freedom to roam and explore new ideas.

- Dislikes overly tight structure that could turn a meeting into a mechanical posting session without priorities.
- May dislike lack of personal contact. This could be dealt with by using video-conferencing, which is almost as simple as a text-only session. A 'whiteboard' system would also allow pictures and drawings to be used and provide opportunities for different kinds of expression.
- The exchange of personal information before meetings would be enjoyed. Having a pre-conference time for catching up on personal information before problem solving begins would make it easy to re-connect with others and find out how things are going. ADs may back the idea of LIFO® Profile exchanges
- Flexibility in formats, colors, variety of font usage would be responded to favorably.
- Playful remarks may be made.
- Attempts will be made to reduce tension – present differences in a good light.

It is clear that this new technology brings with it both opportunities and difficulties for each of the four styles likely to be present in any work team. Team leaders and members using new technology can be much more effective if they know how it will affect each participant. The LIFO® approach which provides a common language can be used to offer new insights and concrete suggestions for making the new technology more acceptable to all of the members of a team. The LIFO® method also predicts the frustrations that each member would naturally experience with this technology and suggests simple changes that make it easier for everyone to contribute more to the collective effort.

APPENDIX I

Sample LIFO® Profiles

The following two samples present scores that would have resulted from taking the complete LIFO® Survey and the written analysis is based on those findings.

Sample 1
LIFO® EXECUTIVE REPORT for INGRID PAULING

LIFO® SCORES

	Supporting Giving	Controlling Taking	Conserving Holding	Adapting Dealing
		Favorable Conditions		
Intention	8	10	5	7
Behavior	9	6	9	6
Impact	5	10	9	6
Total:	22	26	23	19
		Unfavorable or Adverse Conditions		
Intention	7	11	9	3
Behavior	6	11	9	4
Impact	3	9	10	8
Total:	16	31	28	15

Note: Total scores can vary from 9 to 36, Intention, Behavior and Impact scores vary from 3 to 12.

FAVORABLE CONDITIONS

Productive Style

Ms. Pauling approaches situations in a planned and thoughtful way. She is stimulated by problems and challenges and uses a combination of intuitive and analytical assessments. She is not afraid to trust her judgment and experience but is careful about acting prematurely. Achievement of primary organizational goals in an integrated and coordinated manner will be foremost in her priorities. It is important for her to understand what is required, but once acquainted with facts and alternatives, she relies on a systematic approach to implementing required actions. She likes to be busy and involved in a variety of activities and needs to feel a solid sense of accomplishment through her completion of projects. Understanding of goals, purposes and plans in detail will be important to her. Control systems will be used to monitor events. Her overall manner is serious and dedicated.

It is important for her to do work accurately, to spend time to assure that there are no mistakes and that everything can be accounted for. She may prefer a slower pace to assure such control – to do things right! While she can appreciate the urgency of time she would tend to schedule a longer time for decision-making and completion of tasks under normal conditions.

Such an emphasis on proper performance will be communicated to those who work for her. A fairly high degree of structure will be provided for everyone. Instructions will be explicit, along with policies, procedures, and roles defined well. While she will delegate readily she will also follow up assignments closely. There will be invitations to participate in problem-solving discussions and frequent communications provided about issues and expected from staff. Those who are competent, demonstrate responsibility, and execute their assignments thoroughly will be the ones favored. Loyalty, dedication and a cooperative manner are also prized. She will also take interest in helping people develop and will provide guidance when needed. Reviews will be objective and thorough – with a tendency to be more critical than complimentary.

Colleagues should find her serious and cooperatively engaged in group discussions, willing to help, and concerned about the overall welfare of her organization. She will desire planned and coordinated actions and expect time to be spent productively. The factual basis for decision-making will be probed to assure successful solutions. She will want to make sure there is thorough understanding and agreement on actions that require joint commitment.

When she clearly understands the need for change or has been involved in the authorship of her proposed changes she will lend her active support and be highly involved in the detailed planning and implementation. It is important for her to feel that changes are well designed and completely developed. She would prefer to get people involved, assure thorough understanding, and proceed carefully rather than plunging ahead without covering her necessary steps.

Planning, research, strategizing and assessing operations would be aspects of marketing that would attract her attention and interest. Emphasis would be more on operational than customer issues.

Least Preferred Style

Ms. Pauling utilizes a direct and straightforward manner. She is less inclined to use subtle and diplomatic approaches, though she can if alerted to special aspects of a situation. Thus she is likely to proceed more from an objective consideration of business issues from her own viewpoint than from a concern about others' views. She may not realize that the impact of her communications may cause other people to regard her as insensitive. Positive comments and praise are not likely to be used often – which may lower morale. Once committed to an action plan she may not display sufficient flexibility to accommodate changes or to be receptive to different and possibly innovative ideas.

Some Possible Excesses of the Productive Style

She may tend to over plan and spend too much time on detail. A serious and critical manner may make others feel hesitant about sharing partially formed ideas with her even thought they might have potential value for solving problems. Her critical tendencies may also make others feel that she cannot be pleased. Explanations may be so thorough as to be tedious to those who are more action oriented. She may make bright people feel that she doesn't trust their capabilities. Time management may be affected by her concern that everything be carefully checked. Concern about costs may affect willingness to support activities that require developmental effort. Control systems could also be excessive, seeming sometimes more as barriers than as management tools.

UNFAVORABLE OR ADVERSE CONDITIONS

Fight Style

When disagreements occur, Ms. Pauling defends her position with tightly reasoned and determined statements. She persists in trying to convince others that her view is correct, confronting flaws in arguments and lack of information in a direct manner. She will probe and question others about points that are not clear and expect them to respond with reasons and facts. Indeed, it is only superior reasoning and better information that will convince her to concede. Such encounters are serious activities – she rarely uses humor or is willing to compromise under such circumstances. Effort is spent more on fighting for her views than listening intently to the opponent's position and empathetically demonstrating understanding.

Conflict can escalate when differences are intense and there are heated emotional exchanges. She will generally be unlikely to give in, creating an impression of stubbornness and resistance to

—

change. When confronting someone who has more power and higher rank, she may become silent and fail to fully reveal her feelings. Silence for her may indicate anger and disagreement.

Stress Style

When faced with pressure, she responds by taking charge, obtaining information about what has happened, planning an effective response, and organizing efforts. She will establish schedules and budgets, follow up closely and take over direction if things are not going as expected. She tends to rely on her own judgment and experience rather than involving others.

When stress is intense, she may over participate in events, undermine delegation, and make heavy demands on others. This is done with a heavy touch, rarely attending to morale and using encouragement and praise to motivate others. She places a heavy load on herself and others until the crisis is resolved.

RECOMMENDATIONS
To those who wish to improve communications with Ms. Pauling

She appreciates people who are responsive to her requests, clear and organized in their presentations, and who can support opinions with solid information. Be direct, sincere and straightforward. Get down to business quickly and don't waste her time. Stress practicality, costs, steps to follow, and expected outcomes. Provide data and recommendations and give her time to think things through. Make sure information cited is accurate – she won't appreciate guesses. If you are unsure, let her know and then get the necessary information. Make sure to keep her up to date on progress. Don't be afraid to ask for help if you need it but don't behave in a dependent way.

She prefers to work for those who value her input, provide

information about significant events, allow for questions, and are clear in their directions.

Under unfavorable conditions, state your views confidently and respectfully, providing detailed information, substantiation, and recommendations. Directly address questions raised. Avoid critical remarks. Once a decision has been made, cease the arguments and support it.

During crisis situations don't raise new issues that aren't relevant to her situation at hand. Instead of raising questions, make suggestions in a positive way. Respond swiftly to requests and demonstrate that you are on top of what is happening. Report any progress failures or emergencies immediately.

What Ms. Pauling can do to improve her communications with others

Ms. Pauling's penchant for detail might not interest those who are more action oriented. They will want her to provide concise, edited reports with bottom-line implications. She will have to shorten explanations and provide detailed data only when questioned. Bright and capable people who will feel that she underestimates their ability might also resent lengthy explanations and instructions. Communications therefore should be tailored to her audience. It would pay to determine how much others know, what they perceive and feel before talking with them. In addition, Ms. Pauling should be alert to reactions and deal with those, as well as the points she wants to make. Before formulating policies and procedures she should talk about them with those likely to be affected by such changes. This would help to increase their acceptance and also make sure they will deal with concerns that are raised.

Ms. Pauling also ought to be alert to the organizational climate and values that characterize others' interests, especially when dealing with outside departments and agencies. This would be especially critical when consulting. Listening and encouraging others to talk about their feelings may reveal important information that wouldn't be obtained otherwise, as well as build rapport.

Criticism needs to be tempered with praise to encourage others and reinforce desirable performance. She should let others know what she finds valuable in what they say and do.

Intention, Behavior and Impact

When examining the consistency between these three factors in Ms. Pauling's profile, some discrepancies appear. For example, it seems that people do not see her as helpful and interested as she would like, despite the fact that she tries to behave in such a manner. One wonders whether this is due to the high involvement in control – stating views strongly and, perhaps, trying to help by telling rather than suggesting.

Equally interesting is the fact that, although the frequency of controlling behavior is much lower than the intent, people still see her as very controlling. This may also be influenced by the low involvement in Adapting-Dealing behavior – Ms. Pauling doesn't temper her remarks with considerations of how others are feeling.

The lack of expression of her own feelings and the objective, serious focus may also influence the perception that she is somewhat more remote and distant.

The intensity of her Controlling-Taking and Conserving-Holding behavior under conflict and stress provides an impression of strength that masks the fact that although Ms. Pauling is sometimes willing to give in, others fail to see that. What is surprising is that people see her as more needful of approval than she seems to want – as if she might be willing to compromise even though she doesn't intend to.

What seems to emerge is the importance of Ms. Pauling providing more information for others about how she feels – for showing more interest in them and their feelings – more involvement in the social sphere of interaction.

SOME OTHER STRENGTH MANAGEMENT®
RECOMMENDATIONS

Freer delegation with less supervision could encourage more initiative of staff members as well as free some of Ms. Pauling's time. Tighter structuring of schedules to increase the pace of decision-making would also be helpful in an organization that is undergoing rapid change. Although likely to establish sound procedures, she should examine them periodically to see if they are keeping pace with the developmental stage of the organization.

Disagreements could be easier to handle by establishing criteria for acceptance of a proposal and obtaining agreement to those yardsticks in advance of discussion. This could reduce some of the tense aspects and enable freer expression of views.

During stressful situations, seeking advice from expert sources could relieve tension as well as provide fresh perspectives on what is happening. It could also avoid giving the impression that she has a closed mind. She should look at how she is delegating under stress so as not to have to spend so much energy doing things herself or undermining her delegation.

Sample 2
LIFO® EXECUTIVE REPORT for KEN HENDERSON

LIFO® SCORES

	Supporting Giving	Controlling Taking	Conserving Holding	Adapting Dealing
Favorable Conditions				
Intention	5	10	7	8
Behavior	6	8	9	7
Impact	4	12	6	8
Total:	14	30	22	23
Unfavorable or Adverse Conditions				
Intention	5	9	7	9
Behavior	7	10	5	8
Impact	6	11	8	5
Total:	18	30	20	22

Productive Style

Mr. Henderson uses a decisive and assertive approach in most situations. He is accustomed to sizing up a situation quickly, intuitively assessing what is involved and deciding what action is required. His background and experience are trusted as guides for decision-making. Mr. Henderson enjoys working in a varied and demanding job situation where there are opportunities to assume responsibility and influence the course of results. Spontaneity and swift responsiveness, along with an optimistic and confident attitude are highly characteristic. Planning is largely informal; he relies on others to sketch out the details involved and to execute them. Communications are confident, outgoing and sociable.

Staff members find him a vigorous, enthusiastic and demanding boss who is willing to delegate a lot once they have demonstrated their competence. They are expected to invest a great deal of effort and commitment to their assignments and be willing to accomplish things competently and relate smoothly with others. Mr. Henderson makes clear decisions and provides a fair amount of feedback. Initiative is highly prized by him.

Colleagues experience an active and energetic person during group discussions who offers his own ideas readily and enjoys the give-and-take of argumentation. Mr. Henderson is concerned that meetings are productive and optimize the use of available time. He makes efforts to express ideas in an optimistic and positive manner. He prefers to be decisive about issues and cover a lot of ground.

Generally, Mr. Henderson views change as challenging and full of opportunity, and he welcomes the chance to problem-solve issues involved. Nonetheless, he doesn't treat all proposals for change equally: he has to see changes as pragmatic and beneficial. He responds more favorably if he has a key role in implementing the new change. It is important for him to feel that his ideas are welcomed during the formulation process. Arbitrarily imposed changes might be resisted.

If involved with marketing, there would be interest in formulating bold strategies and framing the approaches that would be required. There should be a fair amount of customer sensitivity in his orientation. Detailed market analyses and research would be less likely to engage his interest.

Least Preferred Style

Disciplined and highly systematic approaches are least likely to be employed by Mr. Henderson. He tends to be more intensely involved in holistic aspects, and therefore, he may overlook or ignore some details of information and procedures while executing his plans. His instructions and communications might not be as explicit as others would require. Documentation can also suffer.

———

Some Possible Excesses of the Productive Style

Mr. Henderson's actions could be overly impulsive, occasionally failing to consider all of the relevant material and facts. This could be compensated by swift changes when errors are made. Preoccupation with his own views and an assertive manner could cause over participation and domination of discussions. A tendency to become highly involved with everything might cause some time management problems.

UNFAVORABLE OR ADVERSE CONDITIONS

Fight Style

When challenged, or encountering disagreements, he argues strongly for his position, striving to prove his point to win the dispute. He will be quick to defend against criticism. Open confrontation will be respected. He enjoys the give-and-take of argument. However, his typical reaction will be to fight back. His own position is not likely to be conceded readily except to overwhelming data or superior logic. He does not tend to shy away from confrontation, and rather, will be persuasive and try to win over his opponent. He may see opposition more as a challenge than as an insoluble obstacle. Thus, he may even perceive this kind of situation as highly stimulating. If he doesn't win his point readily and it is apparent that conflict is creating antagonism or bad feelings, he will be willing to listen, negotiate, and compromise. He will then be more attentive to the other person's position and the impact of his own statements and actions. He may use humor and a lighter style of approach to relieve tension and promote a more conciliatory mood in his opponent.

When conflict is very intense, he may become too defensive, geared to win, and come across so forcefully that less assertive members of the group may not feel free or comfortable enough to express their views. This, in turn, may produce defensiveness, discourage people from fully cooperating in problem solving, and would prevent potentially valuable information from being shared and utilized. Rather than a problem-solving situation, Mr. Henderson may, in excess, perceive a disagreement as a win-or-lose battle.

Stress Style

When facing crisis or emergency conditions, he will attempt to maintain a swift, directive, and organized approach, especially when the situation is familiar. Confronting unfamiliar conditions, however, he will assess the situation carefully, establish priorities, and develop a well-articulated plan of action. He will personally direct efforts, often taking on a large portion of direct task responsibilities himself in order to restore everything to order as soon as possible. Communication demands will be heavy and he will review closely the work in progress. Despite pressures, he will try to be encouraging and attentive to morale during these times. Although preferring to utilize well-tested methods, he would experiment with more innovative approaches if the former were not succeeding.

When stress is intense, particularly when fatigued, he may try to do too many things himself, diffusing his efforts and possibly limiting his effectiveness. He could be nitpicking and hypercritical, and as a result, undermine delegation by undercutting subordinates' confidence in themselves to deliver what he requires. He may be prone to promising too much without being able to deliver it, disappointing those who were dependent upon him.

RECOMMENDATIONS

To those who wish to improve communications with Mr. Henderson

Under favorable conditions, Mr. Henderson will be responsive to messages that are clear, concise, and to the point. A presentation style that conveys enthusiasm, confidence, and stresses challenges and opportunities will be favorably received. Some peripheral concerns would be issues regarding quality, long-term goals and objectives, and the general acceptance of proposals by others in the organization. Avoidance of long, highly detailed presentations of data and documentation is important. Bottom-line impacts, headlines and major issues would be more effective to retain his interest. Indicating a willingness to accept responsibility and exhibiting initiative and competence will be crucial. However, the final decision should be left to him.

When in disagreement, it would be important to state one's views with confidence and respect. However, an unyielding position with no room for compromise would lead to a protracted argument.

What Mr. Henderson can do to improve communication with others

Mr. Henderson would benefit from a more organized and systematic presentation style. At times he may lack focus, jumping from idea to idea without laying sufficient groundwork and linkage for others to follow his train of thought. Spending additional time developing an organized sequence of ideas and presentation of facts, information, and documentation would increase his credibility (particularly if interacting with others who have a more Conserving-Holding orientation). When delegating, communicating requirements and expectations explicitly will help prevent misunderstanding and increase his level of satisfaction with end results.

—

When experiencing crisis situations, communicating a sense of trust and faith in subordinates' or co-workers' competence will help establish a greater sense of team spirit, as well as convey the feeling that delegation is genuine.

Intention, Behavior, and Impact

Generally, there is a high degree of congruence in Mr. Henderson's communications. Under Favorable Conditions, one wonders, though, why he feels he may not be perceived as helpful and considerate as he intends to be. Given the high emphasis on control, his assertive manner may mask those Supporting-Giving intentions. Sometimes he may really be softer than he sounds. Another possibility is that when he tries to be helpful his suggestions sound directive. Under Unfavorable Conditions, the Supporting-Giving and Adapting-Dealing areas are also ones where misunderstandings can arise. Although Mr. Henderson uses behaviors that indicate concessions occasionally, it may be hard for others to realize that is the case. Also, despite the fact he wants his actions to meet with approval and do behave in ways he feels are empathic, it doesn't come off as well as he might hope. The aura of the high Controlling-Taking emphasis may make it harder for people to perceive the other intents. Perhaps, some diminution in tone and more emphasis on the other person may enable the other orientations to be perceived more accurately.

Some Additional Strength Management® Recommendations

Mr. Henderson may find it useful to pay more attention to detail in favorable conditions. An assistant who is strong in administrative functioning would help plug organizational gaps. Use of priority rankings, checklists, systematic procedures, and schedules are recommended.

In stress situations, increased emphasis on delegation and group effort would be beneficial, particularly if he is experiencing time management problems. Although he might still be concerned with team morale, there is likely to be a lesser emphasis on team cohesiveness and team functioning. At those times he should direct some effort towards fostering greater team cooperation and interdependence. Doing so could make it easier for him to cope with crisis situations and decrease the stress he experienced when dealing with them.

Overall Considerations for Consulting Activities

He should work well in situations where needs are apparent and clients are needful of suggestions and direction, demonstrating confidence and relating in a friendly manner. With more decisive clients Mr. Henderson may not listen enough and allow clients to solve their own problems. In finding solutions he may accept too quickly the first one that seems feasible, rather than examine alternatives carefully – he can be too quick to implement without planning in depth.

When clients show resistance, Mr. Henderson may fail to acknowledge what they are saying and try too hard to prove his own points, preferring a "hard sell" kind of approach. Yet, in difficult situations, he can stand up firmly to people who are aggressive and trying to test his mettle, earning respect from those who favor a Controlling-Taking style.

While he assumes responsibility readily and invests a lot in what he does, Mr. Henderson may be too reliant on his own abilities and reluctant to seek advice and guidance when it could be helpful.

APPENDIX II

LIFO® APPLICATIONS

As you will have realized, the LIFO® philosophy can be extended to a wide variety of applications in both your work and personal lives.

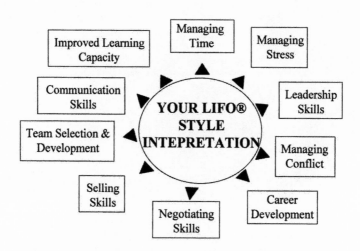

THE VERSALITY OF THE LIFO® METHOD

Experience with LIFO® applications over the past 30 years have demonstrated its usefulness across an even wider range of relationship and personal development needs including the following:

- Marital Relations
- Learning Styles
- Teaching Styles
- Hiring and Selection Processes
- Strategy Formulation

In fact, there are specialized LIFO® surveys that address the specific nature of many of these applications.

APPENDIX III

GETTING INFORMATION ABOUT THE LIFO® METHOD

The LIFO® organization has trained representatives located in more than 20 countries. LIFO® surveys and materials have been translated into 13 languages.

In the United States, inquiries for learning more about using the LIFO® Method for yourself, in your workplace or for other purposes can be addressed to:

BCon LIFO® International Inc.
Suite 660
11111 Santa Monica Boulevard
Los Angeles, CA 90025
Phone number: 1 310-473-2133
Fax number: 1 310-473-2313
Email: www. information@bcon-lifo.com
Websites: akintl.com
          bcon-lifo.com

In addition, you can obtain information about LIFO® programs, materials and services can be obtained from agency offices in many parts of the world:

Argentina	Lic. Adrianna Piccardo
Chile, Uru.	LORE Inc.
	Uruguay 1061 5° 65 (ACA 1016) Buenos Aires

Tel/Fax: (54)11-4813-2676
Mob: (54)11-154028-0721
apiccardo@fibertel.com.ar

Australia   Peter Renfrew, Managing Director
RYM Consulting Group
29 Panorama Way
Sanctuary Lakes 3030
Australia
Tel: (61)-3-9395-2142
prenfrew@ozemail.com.au

Benelux   MATCH, bv, Annelique De Jong, Managing
Director
Marathon 9c
1213 Hilversum
The Netherlands
Tel: (31)-35-683-47-90
Fax: (31)-35-683-05-80
a.de.jong@match-bv-nl
Karel Adriaensen (Belgium)
Karel.Adriansen@planetintrtrnet.be

Canada: Linda Wiens, Managing Director
Quetico Centre
P.O. Box 1000
Atikokan, Ontario
Canada, POT 1Co
Tel: (807)-929-3511
Fax: (807)-929-1106
qcmail@queticocentre.com
Shirley Murray
1580 Kings Street W.
Toronto, Ont. M6K1J2
Tel: (416)-533-3239
Fax: (416)-533-1424
samurray2@yahoo.com

China and
Taiwan: Dr. Dz-Lyang Chen
              East-West Management Consulting, Inc.
              1602 Hongkong Plaza
              283 Middle Huaihai Rd.
              Shanghai, China PC:200021
              Tel: (86)-21-63906236
              Fax: (86)-21-63906233
              ewtaiwan@ms21.hinet.net
              gary@ew-hrm.com

Germany: Dr. Rene Bergermaier
              LPC LIFO® Products & Consulting
              Nymphenburger Str. 148
              80634 München, Germany
              Tel: (49)-89-130-6800
              Fax: (49)-89-161711
              Rene.Bergermaier@lifoproducts.de

Indonesia: Linda Hairgrove, Frank Hairgrove, Peter
              Hidayat
              Pegasus Consulting Group
              Setrasari Mail B1-6
              Jl.lr Sutami Bandung 40164, Indonesia
              lindalee@securenym.net

Japan: Hiroko Yamane
              Business Consultants, Inc.
              2-2-1 Yaesu, Chuo-Ku
              Tokyo 104-0028
              Japan
              Tel: (81)-03-3274-2591
              Fax: (81)-03-3281-4353
              h-yamane@bcon.co.jp

Korea: Ilgi Kim, Contact Person
              BCon Korea, Inc.
              Suite 516, City Air Terminal Bldg.
              159-6, Samsung-Dong, Gangnam-Gu

Seoul 135-726, Korea
Tel: (82)-2-6242-2591
Fax: (82)-2-6241-2592

Middle
East : Kiki Magireli
Inter Associates Ltd
34 Townsend Road
Ashford, Middlesex TW15 3PS
United Kingdom
Tel: (44)-1784 – 255896
Fax: (44)-1784-423-995
k.magireli@talk21.com
Kenneth Pasternak
Inter Associates Ltd.
Mechelininkatu 19A17
Helsinki 00100
Finland
Tel: (358)-9-454-3325
Fax: (358)-9-454-3326
pasternak@kolumbus.fi

Norway and
Sweden: Betty Forbis, Gregory Metzler, Ingjerd Nomme,
Birger Bertheussen, Scott Forbis
Barnum Associates International
6 Flintlock Roadx
Lexington, MA 02420
Tel: (781)-862-3008
Fax: (781)-861-6940
betty.forbis@barnumassociates.com
Ingjerd Nomme
Barnum Associates Norway
Hvidstenv. 25
P.O. Box 337
1396 BILLINGSTAD
Tel.: (47) 66 98 06 80

	Fax.: (47) 66 98 10 88
	Mob. (47) 93 02 10 04
	barnum@online.no
Romania:	Alexandru Molnar & Marius Popa
	Consilium s.r.l.
	Str. Prot. G. Popovici nr 8/A
	1900 Timisoara, Rümanien
	Office Consilium
	Tel: 40-56-221501
	Fax: 40-56-196994
	alex@consilium.ro & marius@consilium.ro
Russia	Dr. Marina F. Baranoff & Tatjiana
	Kuznetsova
	308 310 Skakovaya str.
	17 Business Center
	125 040 Moscow, Russia
	Tel: (007)-095-946 15 48
	Tel: (007)-095-945 18 76
	almars@mir.mik.ru
Slovakia	Reinhold Hofmann, Managing Director
	HIC Slovakia s.r.o.
	Matejkova 57
	84105 Bratislava, Slovakia
	Tel: (421)-2-6541-1082
	Fax: (421)-2-6541-1084
	Reinhold.hofmann@hic.sk
So. Africa	Laurie Hall, Managing Director
	Garry Whyte Associates, Ltd.
	4th Floor, Hyde Park Corner
	Jan Smuts Avenue
	Hyde Park 2196, South Africa
	Tel: (27)-11-325-4415
	Fax: (27)-11-325-4113 mail@gwa.co.za

Switzerland   Jacques Brochon, Managing Director
              Personnel Management Consultants
              Rue du Bugnon 4
              Ch 1299 Crans-Celigny, Switzerland
              Tel: (41)-22-776-46-94
              Fax: (41)-22-776-03-07
              Jacques@directionplus.com
United   Bridget Biggar, Managing Director
Kingdom   Life Orientations® Limited
              Alwood House
              Alwood Road
              Maidenhead
              Berkshire SL6 4QD, United Kingdom
              Tel: (44)-1628-633101
              Fax: (44)-1628-771268
              action@lifeorientations.com

APPENDIX IV

BIBLIOGRAPHY

Atkins S. The name of your game, Beverly Hills, Ellis & Stewart, 1981, 1999

Atkins, S. & Katcher, A. Getting your team in tune, *Nation's Business*, Mar. 1975

Atkins, S. & Katcher, A. Six lessons in leadership, Los Angeles, Bcon LIFO® International Inc., 2002

Atkins, S. & Katcher A. The LIFO® Life Orientations Survey, Beverly Hills, Atkins-Katcher Associates, 1967, Bcon LIFO® International, Inc., 2001

Atkins, S. & Katcher, A. The LIFO® General Applications Workbook, Beverly Hills, Atkins-Katcher Associates, 1967, Allan Katcher International, Inc. 1979, Bcon-LIFO® International, Inc, 2001

Belbin, R. M. Management Teams, Oxford, Butterworth-Heinemann, 1981, 1999

Bergamini, C. W. Que tipo de executivo voce e? *Exame, Sao Paulo*, 86:87-91, 1974

Bergamini, C. W. LIFO®: A Brazilian experience. *Industrial Training International*, London, 11 (7-8): 239-40, jul-aug, 1976

Buckingham, M. & Clifton, D. O. Now discover your strengths, New York, The Free Press, 2001

Czichos, R. Profils managen sich selbst, Munich, Ernst Reinhardt, 2001

Dixon, M. How strength can be an executive's ruin. *Financial Times*, 23, Nov. 1978

Drucker, P. The practice of management, New York, Harper & Row, 1954

Fromm E. Man for himself, Greenwich, Fawcett, 1947

Katcher, A. A importancia de ser voce meus. Sao Paulo, Editoria Atlas, 1989

Katcher, A. Intention, behavior and impact, Los Angeles, Bcon-LIFO® International, Inc. 2001

Katcher, A. Applying the LIFO® Method to organizational effectiveness., *Industrial Training International*, London, 11:189-191, 1976

Rogers, C. On becoming a person. Boston, Houghton-Mifflin, 1951

Wainwright, D. The half an hour management style test. *Personnel Management*, 10, 1978

See also the list of articles on the web site www.bcon-lifo.com Go to the link for the documents archive. There are approximately 100 articles on the origin of The LIFO® Method, theory, applications in leadership training, management and organizational.development, recruitment, sales training, conflict and stress management, and team building. Many training exercises are also provided.

Short Biography of Allan Katcher

Dr. Katcher, President of Bcon LIFO® International, Inc. has been a consultant to many of the Fortune 500 companies, including: Cisco, Citicorp, Exxon, General Foods, Household International, Northrop, and Xerox.

His doctorate in psychology was earned at the University of California (Berkeley) and he has taught there, UCLA, Brooklyn College, The California Institute of Technology, and the University of Washington. He has lectured and conducted seminars in more than 20 countries.

Prior to establishing his own consulting firm, he was manager of executive development at Douglas Aircraft Company, head of management development at The System Development Corporation and a human factors scientist at The Rand Corporation.

Short Biography of Kenneth P. Pasternak

Mr. Pasternak is a principle consultant for Inter Associates Ltd. His career has combined corporate banking, project management, management consulting, and training positions with Citibank N.A in New York, London, Helsinki, Istanbul, Brussels, and Jersey, Channel Islands.

In 1992 he joined the European Bank for Reconstruction and Development in London where his team developed training institutions and small business support centers in central and eastern Europe and the former Soviet Union. In 1997 Mr. Pasternak was honored with the title of Academician of the Russian Federation by a consortium of seven leading Russian universities.

Based in Helsinki, Finland since 1996 he has been advising corporations and financial institutions throughout Europe and the USA in the areas of strategy, management development, and cross-cultural communications.